ALOPECIA
OUR STORIES
Living the Bald Life

Presented By
Jamie Elmore

BALife**D** MAGAZINE
"WHEN BALD IS UNIVERSAL"

THANK You So Very Much for Your Support

ALOPECIA: OUR STORIES

Copyright © 2023 by Bald Life Magazine

All rights are reserved. Except as permitted under the U.S. Copyright Act of 1976, no part of the publication may be reproduced, distributed, or transmitted in any form or by any means, or stored in a database or retrieval system without the prior written permission of the publisher.

This book is available in volume for qualifying organizations. Please contact the author's team to inquire via email info@baldlifemagazine.com.

For more information about this book, or speaking engagements please email info@baldlifemagazine.com.

Seattle, WA
Since 2020

ISBN- 9798392400508
For Worldwide Distribution
Printed in the U.S.

TABLE OF CONTENTS

Introduction..v

Foreword..viii

1. Your Crown is Your Glory........................3
   Meet Lisa Ennis

2. Living With Alopecia...........................14
   Meet Natalie Bryant

3. The Little Girl with the Blue Hat..............24
   Meet Sarah Cunha

4. Alopecia Didn't Break Me.......................33
   Meet Enjolé Johnson, Esq.

5. Born to Stand Out..............................44
   Meet Melissa Dogonniuck

6. Redefining the Essence of My Beauty............59
   Meet Makeda James, MPH

7. Finding Joy After Alopecia.....................68
   Meet Erika Hill, MCRP

8. Hair Loss is NOT a Death Sentence..............82
   Meet Angela McCullers

9. The Alchemy of Loving Yourself.................92
   Meet Chloe Bean

10. My First Time at The Wig Store................105
    Meet Delena Thompson

11. Is Love Really Blind?........................112
    Meet the Chaplins

12. The Secrets to Marriage With Alopecia.........129
    Meet the Browns

13. From Lyme to Limeade.........................147
    Meet The Coopers

14. The Mirror...................................164
    Meet Jamie Elmore

INTRODUCTION

"Your story is NOT your story. Your STORY is for someone else!" ~ Jamie Elmore

What is Alopecia?

Alopecia [al-uh-pee-shee-]: an autoimmune disease in which your immune system attacks your hair follicle, and hair loss occurs, usually involving the scalp and, at times, every hair on your body. Alopecia does not discriminate. Alopecia occurs in men and women of all races equally. It can develop at any age. Alopecia does not discriminate. Alopecia areata occurs in 2 percent of the population—6.8 million people in the U.S. and 147 plus people worldwide. Hair loss in women often has a greater impact than hair loss in men because it's socially acceptable for them. The traumatic experience can be the same.

There are several types of Alopecia. I will list nine below.

- Alopecia Areata (Patchy hair loss on the scalp, face, and or body)
- Alopecia Totalis (Hair loss across the entire scalp)
- Alopecia Universalis (Hair loss across the whole body,

including eyebrows, eyelashes, and possibly nose hairs)

- Androgenetic Alopecia (Hair loss that affects the top and front of the scalp)
- Central Centrifugal Cicatricial Alopecia (Scarring Alopecia)
- Chemotherapy Induced Alopecia (Anagen Effluvium)
- Diffused Alopecia Areata (Sudden and unexpected thinning of the hair all over the scalp)
- Frontal Fibrosing Alopecia (A receding hairline that runs along the front and sides)
- Traction Alopecia (Repeated pulling on the hair, braids, weaves, ponytails)

In 1998 I found my first bald spot. In 2004 I was diagnosed with Alopecia. As a woman, salon owner, and hairstylist, I struggled and endured personal trauma from losing my hair. For years I dealt with depression, low self-esteem, and anxiety. I also struggled to embrace my femininity.

After my diagnosis with Alopecia, I was surprised by the lack of resources and support for a worldwide epidemic disease. I was striving to gain back my normalcy. I wanted to create and become a resource for what I wished was accessible when dealing with the post-traumatic effects of Alopecia.

I wanted to heal and help others do the same. I wanted to create a community for men, women, and children where they could experience transformation and support. An internal shift that helps them reach their full potential and how they see and relate to society despite living with Alopecia and hair loss.

As the songwriter, India Arie says, "I am not my hair, I am not this skin, I am the soul that lives within."

I soon began to understand that everything that I went through regarding my Alopecia was bigger than me. God began to give me innovative ways for people to heal.

Thus, the Alopecia Anthology project series was founded. This project gives my Alopecia community opportunities to become authors and share their stories that aim to provide a road map for others to heal and understand that they are not alone. A collaboration book will allow the readers to unlearn societal norms regarding beauty, relationships, and acceptance. This book will empower you to tell your story.

Jamie Elmore ~ Visionary

FOREWORD

Are you ready for some real talk? Because that's exactly what you're going to get on the pages of this book. The stories shared here are not your typical "woe is me" tales of tragedy and despair. No, these are stories of resilience, strength, and courage. These are stories of individuals who have taken what could have been a debilitating condition and turned it into a source of power.

When we think of hair loss, we often think of it as a natural part of aging or as a side effect of medical treatment. But for the millions of people worldwide who live with Alopecia, hair loss is not just a physical change but a deeply personal and emotional experience that can profoundly impact their self-esteem, relationships, and overall quality of life.

Alopecia. It's a word that strikes fear into the hearts of many. It's a word that conjures images of bald patches, wigs, and endless doctor's visits. It's a word that, for many, carries a sense of shame and embarrassment.

In this book, you'll meet individuals who share their stories of living with Alopecia, from the initial shock of diagnosis to the challenges and triumphs of learning to live without hair. They have refused to let Alopecia define them. Through their experiences, we gain a deeper understanding of the complexity and diversity of Alopecia and the ways in which it can affect individuals in unique and unexpected ways.

Despite the challenges they face, the contributors to this book demonstrate remarkable resilience, strength, and courage. They remind us that living with Alopecia is not just about losing hair but about learning to embrace our true selves, no matter what that may look like.

They've embraced their baldness, worn their wigs like crowns, and shown the world what true beauty looks like. They've built careers, families, and friendships in spite of the challenges they've faced. They've lived full, rich lives, and they've done it with a sense of boldness and sass that is truly inspiring.

Whether you are living with Alopecia yourself, know someone who is, or simply want to understand this often-misunderstood condition, this book is a powerful and inspiring testament to the human spirit and the resilience of the human body and mind.

We can stand to learn a lot from each of them.

Precious S. Brown

PRESENTS

ALOPECIA OUR STORIES
Living the Bald Life

BALD. BOLD. BLESSED.

Lisa Ennis

I dedicate my chapter to my sister Shelia Cameron. Shelia, through her illness, gave me the courage to live my bald life. She lost her hair due to chemo, but she never stopped walking boldly. She was so very confident in what she was going through. Shelia here's to you. I am a bald boss because of you.

YOUR CROWN IS YOUR GLORY

"Anyone can be confident with a full head of hair"

~ Unknown author.

As a child my hair was always thin, but with a tight curl. I had so much hair per square inch. My mother used to shampoo my hair with Prell shampoo. How many of you remember Prell? We had well water and no conditioner, but she used Prell. There were no salon visits. When I became a teenager and had a job, the salon became my best friend. I was so proud of my nice and healthy hair. I would cut it, then grow it.

Have you ever heard the quote, "Your hair is your Crown and Glory"? What if you don't have any hair? Where are your Crown and Glory? I began noticing my hair thinning when I was in my early twenties, the time my hair was looking its best ever at first. I actually thought the hairdresser that had done my hair that day left relaxer in my hair, causing it to thin out. I soon came to the reality that I was losing my hair. The truth is that the women on my father's side of the family all wore wigs, and on my mother's side, all had thin spots. There was no way I could escape Alopecia and hair loss. I tried at the onset many methods to camouflage. I would do an individual strand weave, and the spot got bigger (as a Hair Stylist, I knew better). I tried braids, braided weaves, interlocking methods, micro linking; I did whatever I could to hide it when I could no longer camouflage it.

I found it very difficult to find a hairstylist that would take the time and care enough to be creative and work with my lack of hair. Even in my own salon, finding someone that was patient enough to work on my need was challenging. I started feeling like I was bothersome. I did not want to expose myself in front of my staff, let alone clients. I would often get my hair done when the salon was closed. I felt very ashamed and very embarrassed, and my confidence was very shattered. I would often be stood up by a stylist. I would think, "What would I do if I have a client in the morning, a meeting, or church?

I believed God for my healing and miracle (As a woman of faith, I believe God can do anything). I believed that he would stop my follicles from being attacked (that is what was happening) and begin to grow. I was looking for a miracle. After all, he healed the paraplegic man at the pool of Bethesda (John 5:1-5), and he healed the blind man (John9:1-7). I witnessed with my own eyes he was healing one of my fellow church members, extending her leg where she no longer had a limp. Surely, he would heal me.

I felt it was my fault that I didn't have a full head of hair. I was at a church retreat one weekend (I was so looking forward to the retreat). I went to be refreshed, and instead, I was shattered. On the opening night of the retreat, the host Pastor had a woman with a gorgeous head of hair stand up and then asked her to swing her beautiful hair (let me make this clear, as a hairstylist, I was in no way envy nor jealous). Then the pastor scanned the room, seeking others with full heads of hair, and began to ask others to stand and swing their hair. You can imagine how I felt. I felt isolated and alone. Once again, I felt it was my fault that I didn't have hair like the others. I felt I didn't fit in. I also felt that I wasted my time and money going to this retreat. It was totally inappropriate and had nothing to do with what we were there for. I do not believe the pastor did this intentionally, and I don't hold any ill will in my heart.

I became very burden for women with hair loss and or Alopecia, and I wanted to learn more about Alopecia and its effects. I decided to expand my career as a cosmetologist to become a Trichologist, one who specializes in the intense study of hair and scalp conditions. I also learned to make custom wigs and started making my own wigs. I would get it cut and style it myself. During my study as a Trichologist, I studied the cycle of hair, where hair will grow (anagen stage), the growth stops (catagen stage), and when the hair follicles are completely at rest (telogen stage). I would get so excited to get to class to see what I would learn new. This education was way beyond beauty school. In my studies is where I found out the type of Alopecia that I have - Cicatricial Alopecia, also called scarring Alopecia. This type of Alopecia is usually found in women of color. My hair grows everywhere on my head except the top center.

I began my studies as a Trichologist in 2015 and became certified officially in 2019, the year my dear sister passed away from pancreatic cancer. Unlike me, my sister had a full head of hair. Her hair started to fall out due to her chemo, and she became completely bald. I used my clippers to cut the little stubbles that were left on top of her head. After cutting her hair, I took the clippers to my head and then shaved it. When I came out of the bathroom and showed my new look to my sister, we really looked like twins. No one knew that I was bald except my sister. I was still wearing my wigs and other hair adornments.

In 2020 a dear friend (who suffers from Alopecia) invited me to join this live on Facebook. A lady was going to be interviewing someone with Alopecia. I was intrigued. The interview spoke to me. I joined to listen to the conversation. I started smiling, and for once, I felt I wasn't alone. The conversation drew me in. I was leaning forward, thinking that, finally, others understood my story. There were so many bald women tuned in. I started looking at their pictures and thought these ladies were absolutely beautiful. I became social media friends with many of them. I looked at the before pictures with their wigs and weaves, and when I saw their bald pictures, I thought everyone looked absolutely stunning without hair. They were all beautiful. It was my first time thinking bald was beautiful. I started wondering what do I really look like with this bald head? What was my head shape? Although I cut my hair when my sister was having chemo, I never really looked at myself. I was so curious to see my shaved head but was in so much fear. I thought, "I am a cosmetologist; how would this look with me having no hair? What would people think? How comfortable will they be with me as their stylist?" Revealing my baldness was a bold move for me.

Right before seeing Jamie (the Visionary of this book) on Facebook, I read about Congresswoman Ayanna Pressley, who had just shaved her head. I received a text from someone stating, "Read the article on Ayanna Pressley." I did and thought how brave and working with the congress. The person didn't know that I had already done it; I had already cut my hair.

The fear started to grip me, but I wanted to overcome it. I started encouraging myself, saying, "Well, clients won't have to guess what my hair looks like. When I travel with friends, I wouldn't have to hide my wigs under the sink any longer (I did that y'all). I could have options; I can wear a wig, hair accessories, or wear nothing. I realized that when I go public and reveal, I have to make it big. So, I scheduled a photo shoot. Then I called one of my besties and shared with her what I was about to do. She encouraged me and said, "Go for it".

The photo shoot took place at my brother-in-law's office. My brother-in-law, nieces, and nephews came as moral support. My nieces helped me into my clothes and encouraged me to smile or not to smile. It was an exciting time. The five of them were so supportive. We made it a family affair.

In January 2021, I did the big reveal. I posted pictures of my bald-headed self on Facebook and in a Newsletter to the clients. I asked God for healing, and he did exactly what I was asking, not the way in which I wanted, but he healed me. I found a tribe of people that look like me, and I felt that I belong. I regained my confidence. I didn't have this looming over me. I faced my truths and accepted that I was a woman living with Alopecia. Hair did not and does not describe who I am. I am beautiful inside and out with hair, without hair, with make-up, and without make-up. I am beautiful. I am not my hair, and my hair is not me. I am Free, free, free, free. Most of all, I have the option of wearing my headgear, which includes accessories, wigs, weaves, and wraps. I truly have options. I am no longer shamed. It is not my fault that I have the autoimmune disease Alopecia. I feel so much freedom. God has given me many gifts, and growing my hair naturally was not one of them.

Someone may be reading my story and they say, "Well, I will not be shaving my head." I say, "That is totally fine. Everyone is not in the same place. I am in no way saying that you should shave, heck I am a hairstylist and believe in wearing wigs. If that is your comfortability, I support you." My next mission is to be a voice in letting women know that they are beautiful. Coaching them into living their best life with their condition. Hair or no Hair.

I know from experience what it feels like not knowing where to fit in and where to go for help. I know the shame and that hair loss can be overwhelming and, truthfully, lead to depression. Just know that you are not alone, and hair loss is not your fault. Bald is now in. I get so many compliments, especially from men.

Living with Alopecia has prompted me to formulate my own line of scalp and hair loss products scheduled to be released in early 2023. The line is a holistic hair loss and scalp line. Remember earlier I stated that it was very hard to find someone that was sensitive enough to take care of my hair and scalp? I will now hire and train people that have a heart and sensitivity for women with hair loss. The stylist will be trained in Trichology. The line of products that is launching in 2023 is named after my deceased mother and sisters. The name, well, I thought you would never ask, is J'Roshe Cosmetics, (J) Joan, (She) Shelia, and (Ro) Rochic. J'Roshe' is a holistic line of products, including vitamins and scalp ointment. May the memories of my three angels be embedded in my heart forever.

As I close this chapter, I want you to know that I believe nothing is by coincidence. I believe in appointed times. You're reading this story at your appointed time. I just ask, after reading my story, that you are really careful about how you address a person with Alopecia. After my big reveal, I had lunch with a few friends. They were so anxious to talk about my new journey. So many questions. One friend kept addressing me as bald. Well, I was offended and responded to her in a brash tone, "It's called Alopecia." Being bald in public was new for me, and my full healing had not taken place. Hair loss is traumatizing. Please don't say to people your bald or your bald head. As a woman living with Alopecia, the autoimmune disease, calling a person bald is very offensive. Now a person living with Alopecia calling another a baldie is ok. However, it is not ok for anyone else to call me or any other living with Alopecia bald. It's Alopecia. I am also a big proponent of including everyone. I ask that you be sensitive to everyone in your company and include them in. #BE INCLUSIVE OF EVERYONE.

My Bald is my crown, it is my glory, and it is absolutely beautiful.

> "There is nothing more rare, nor more beautiful, than a woman being unapologetically herself, comfortable in her perfect imperfection. That is the true essence of beauty."
>
> - Dr. Steve Maraboli

I Live the Bald Life!

Meet Lisa Ennis

Ms. Lisa Ennis is a native of Crofton, Maryland. She is the owner of **Eccentric's The Salon** and **Meet Lisa Ennis Concierge and Consulting**. Ms. Ennis, also known as the "*S.H.I.F.T. Strategist*" is favored for her candid and constructive way, which is also matched with solutions, sound advice, and resources. Ms. Ennis is the author of Visions "Your Blueprint for Business Success" volume 1 and 2; a staff training and development manual for salons, day spas, barber shops, and any start-up business and 40 Ways to Shoestring Market Your Salon (marketing ideas to build your beauty business).

Ms. Ennis is the creator of the Nail Technician School at the Anne Arundel Community College, where she also serves as an Adjunct Professor.

Ms. Ennis is a recent graduate of Goldman's Sach10K Small Business Program. She received a Certificate in Trichology from the World Trichology Society in 2019. She received her Bachelor of Arts in Business Management from UCLA Anderson School of Management in 2006. She also received her Cosmetology license from the International Beauty School in Maryland in 1985. She is a workshop speaker and serves on several boards as an advisor member as well as she mentors young women and other budding entrepreneurs. Her passion for desiring to see others *S.H.I.F.T.*; their mindsets and start enjoying the lifestyle that was intentionally created for us. One of Ms. Ennis' slogan "Passion + Purpose= Provision".

Natalie Bryant

I dedicate my chapter to my mother. I want to thank her for her unwavering love, support, and sacrifice towards my journey with Alopecia. It was her mission to find help, a cure and healing for her child.

LIVING WITH ALOPECIA

"You may live in the world as it is, but you can still work to create the world as it should"

~Michelle Obama

At the age of 5, something struck me. It would divide, conquer, and leave its sting at the hand of my young mother with two sickly children, doctor-to-doctor visits, and a bunch of unanswered questions. My pillow would hold the grip of my shedding hair and the tear stains of my mother's cry. Knowing she could never stop her baby's pain. Going from curly locks to a completely bald head.

A Mothers Tale

Until her hair loss, Natalie was this happy little girl. However, she was too young to understand what was happening to her. When once the happiest child on earth reverted to a quiet, timid little individual, I was in pain as a mother. I could not explain to her what was happening in fear of not even knowing what was going on myself. The doctor's visits would grow, the numerous tests would expand, and the number of doctors became too many to count. My baby was the talk of the day. She was sat in the middle of the room surrounded by white coats, note taking, poking, and prying with repetitive questions that seemed to last a lifetime. I took the sound advice of my grandmother to eventually get my daughter to Atlanta with her father and seek the doctors there at Grady Hospital, whom my grandmother had relationships with.

Natalie went through extended hospital stays, blood tests, and scalp biopsies to still sit with unanswered questions. The doctor only gave me, *"Ma'am, we have reviewed all the tests, and we have no answers. We've consulted with our Los Angeles colleagues, who state your daughter has Alopecia, something too rare to treat in Atlanta."* Without hope, I did what was in my child's best interest as we began the relocation journey. It was not easy for a 24-year-old mother with two small children to revamp my thoughts and life to do what was necessary to get help for my daughter. It was not the plan for my daughter to be gawked at, bullied, or tormented at such a young age. She went from wearing scarves to withdrawing from society. At this point, my motherly instinct kicked in again, and I had to protect her at all costs. As we arrived in Los Angeles and settled in, I could see my baby changing for the worst right before my eyes. It was something. I could not prepare her for life ahead. Only time would tell. This would be when my daughter was diagnosed with Alopecia Areata, with no further treatment or cure. I was told there was no guarantee that Natalie's hair would regrow. The next phase of life would begin for my daughter.

Natalie's View

I was the butt of all jokes. I became the "it" girl of bullying and was teased as the teacher's pet because I feared the children in school. It was either me constantly hiding inside the bathroom stalls at school or my brother being hauled to the principal's office for fighting for the protection of his sister. We were kids (my brother was 10, and I was 7) made to grow up fast. I remember playing on the playground alone or with my imaginary friend because kids thought I had a disease, and if they played with me, they would catch it. I went home crying daily, vowing never to return to school. My mother, not knowing what to do, wanted to help me. So, I was sent to a school for children with disabilities. At that point, I believed they were just like me. There was no one there that would make me fill indifferent. My mother gives credit to her faith in God for my progress, happiness, and way back into society.

These would be the most exciting years of my life, no bullying, no crying, no hiding, or kids being mean and not playing with me. I was often asked by the kids at my new school,

"Why are you here? You seemed normal to me." Afraid of not being accepted after telling the truth, I would make up a story. I was the happiest kid as I transitioned from scarves to pigtail wigs and gained many friends. The world was mine. In the next phase of my journey, I would end up on the west side of town. I was ecstatic to be there, and I even made a friend. He was brown skinned, walked with a limp, and had patches from hair loss. As time went by, I asked him what had happened to him. He explained that he was in a fire and had been burned. That's when I told him about having Alopecia. He would become my forever friend.

> *"When you mistreat someone, you view the part of you that lacks love." ~Princess Tilda*

As I entered the 5th grade, I changed schools. And the transition was a little bit easier. I did not experience that much bullying. However, everyone was curious about my hair and why I wore a wig. My junior high school was fun. I played in the band and excelled in all my classes. My brother was around but did not have to be on bodyguard duty. Life as a preteen was getting easy. I met a boy who was interested in me, I thought. As time passed, he played a trick on me and pulled my wig off in front of some neighborhood friends.

I was heartbroken, and boy, did it show. I cried all night as my mother comforted me until my brother got home. All I could hear him say was *"what is wrong with you?"* My mother told him what had happened, and he couldn't leave it like this. Later, when I asked what he did to that boy, my brother said, "He pulled your hair, so I pulled his." My brother was always my savior, my superhero. My mother saw the strain and toll it took on him, and she made a drastic decision to remove me from the public school to a private school where I would have family support. I went to a school that not only showed love to me but also showed love to my single mother, who was raising me and my siblings on her own.

The 9th grade appeared, and the next phase of my life was to begin as a high schooler. It was a new world and different scenery, where kids were mature, fun, and all over the place. I met my brother there, but I didn't have to lay my burdens on him this time. We both were active at school. He was a player on the football team, and I began my nursing career. I was on the African student union and contemplating cheerleading but declined, fearing my wig flying off. I remember the day as it was today. I was on my way to chemistry class, and as I got to the top of the stairs, it happened. My wig went flying across the room, and the laughter seemed like continuous roars. However, I became immune to the inevitable. I had grown up, and I didn't go running to my brother (however, he found out and put the word out that no one was to ever touch his sister in any form, and it was settled). I picked my wig up, put it back on my head, and continued to class. Time had flown by. Twelfth grade was here, prom, and then graduation time.

> *"The greatest discovery of all time is that a person can change his future by merely changing his attitude"* ~ *Oprah Winfrey*

And just like that, I had gone from being an adolescent, preteen, and teenager to being an adult. This time was the beginning of another level of life gone haywire. I had become a woman. This part of my journey would embark on a new diagnosis. Alopecia Universalis, anemia, thalassemia, lichens sclerosis, low potassium, and dermatomyositis. Adulthood brought on a different type of bullying in the form of sickness, hospitalization, and constant referrals to specialists to help me along the way. I can never turn back the hand I was dealt, but I've grown, taken ownership, and established a patterned way of life.

My sister, Rose, has supported me thus far (She Is My Sisters Keeper). She took over where my brother left off. She says, *"This is a cruel world, and you must be protected."* Being my biggest fan, my defender, my hospital advocate, and my hair Stylist (who made my wigs), she spoke up for me in my timid, shy moments. I know her to have my best interest at heart. She credits me to be one of her best friends. And she is mine also. Being nine years younger, she remembers my hospital visits/stays, treatments, and school bullying. As I became older, I experienced the aftermath and the scars it left behind. Moving forward, Natalie comes out of her shell and turns her hurt into Victory.

My best friend would describe me as strong, resilient, and fearless. He stated, *"Her condition never held her back or stopped her from being who God needed her to be. She embraces the inevitable, sometimes struggling in silence. Yet, she is still strong, resilient, and fearless."*

So many people cross our paths in life, and for some, we hope they stay in our life forever. Another one of my best friends, Desiree said, *"Natalie is beautiful inside and out, with a bright beaming smile."* We would travel, shop, and eat together. However, I knew it was something oddly different about my friend. I never saw someone with such perfectly styled hair. I mean, not a strand out of place. It would be 16 years into our friendship she mustered up the amazing strength to let me know she had Alopecia. *"I have seen Natalie embrace her truth, bringing awareness with determination, compassion, and commitment to bring awareness to Alopecia."*

My daily routine is to look in the mirror and do away with self-doubt by knowing who I am. I practice daily affirmations, self-care, and I push myself to be the best version of me. I still have triggers, fear of the unknown in a relationship, and having to prove myself as a woman living with an autoimmune disease and the challenges it brings. I stand on God, daily affirmations, family, and my love for fashion, coping with the struggle of an image that was not made for me "But To Help Someone Else." At 50, I look for nothing in return from Alopecia. While it's busy doing its job, I will continue doing mine by speaking loud and bold about Alopecia, sharing with others on self-care and how to protect your immune system and trust the process.

"45 is the New 5, living 45 years with Alopecia."

Affirmations for YOU!

- I release the past and trust that everything is happening for my greatest good.

- I am determined to cure my wounds, soul, mind, and see things differently.

- It is time to move ahead to discover the purpose of my existence and own my truth.

Meet Natalie Bryant

Natalie A. Bryant was born in Jacksonville, FL, on January 12th, 1973. She is currently residing in Los Angeles. Natalie is a healthcare professional who loves to care for others.

Natalie believes this passion for people was handed down from her grandmother, who also worked in healthcare. Even more than that, "it is God's calling for her that turned into a deeper passion." He gave her the gift, passion, and love for human beings.

She is an avid volunteer for organizations such as UCLA, Red Cross, Los Angeles Mission (Thanksgiving and Christmas), City of Inglewood voters' registration, Zeta Amicae food and clothing drive, Breast Cancer run-walk marathon, and New Antioch COGIC (Thanksgiving giveaway).

Natalie owns and operates a hospitality business and Co-owns a balloon design business with her sister (Sisters Who Design). Her family and inner circle are her heart pieces. They are affectionately called "My squad is Blessed."

Natalie is a powerful force and uses her positive attitude to encourage and uplift others. Despite embarking on her 45th year living with Alopecia, she has had total hair loss all over her body.

Her greatest fear was she would never be accepted by society. Yet she is reminded of the late Maya Angelou's quote ... "I've learned that people will forget what you said, people will forget what you did, but people will never forget how you made them feel."

Sarah Cunha

I dedicate my story to my grandmother, Patricia Ross, a woman who taught me to "never let someone make me feel down" and instilled in me the core values I've used to navigate through difficult times. Her undying love made me feel seen and heard. My grandmother taught me to have a voice and to use it when standing up for myself and what I believe in. I am so grateful for the strength she gave me in my younger years and continues to give me now as my guardian Angel.

THE LITTLE GIRL WITH THE BLUE HAT

"You may shoot me with your words, you may cut me with your eyes, you may kill me with your hatefulness, but still, like air, I'll rise." - Maya Angelou.

What would it be like to love yourself so fiercely that nothing anyone could say would impact how secure you are in your own body and mind? Have you ever wondered what believing in yourself really looks like? The quote above, pulled from a poem by Maya Angelou, is my favorite. When I was a little girl, my father gave me her book, "And Still, I Rise," which got me through many years of bullying. At the end of some nights, as I brushed away my tears and wondered if anybody cared about me, I would whisper, *"Still, I'll rise."*

When I was six-year-old, I wore a blue hat to school. My classmates would ask, *"how come you get to wear a hat to school when hats aren't allowed?"* I would respond with, *"I don't know"* and look at my feet with sadness because I did know why. Because of Alopecia, I had no hair. The blue hat was a desperate attempt to avoid excessive attention and just be like the other kids.

Five years later, I would walk through the school halls with a wig on my head and be asked, *"are you wearing a wig?"* With embarrassment written all over my face, I would respond, *"No, absolutely not."* Once again, I would stare at my feet and keep my head down. At lunchtime, I would sit in a bathroom stall instead of in a cafeteria full of eyes staring at me. I tried making friends but went about it the wrong way. I would tell a lie after lie. I would deny wearing a wig' even though classmates could tell. I had no eyebrows or eyelashes, but when asked about it, I would respond, *"they're just blonde and really light,"* as if that was believable. I struggled to find my place and eventually kept to myself because I would rather be alone than be myself.

I also dreaded coming to school in the morning because I knew my bully would be waiting for me when I walked in. My bully would stick gum on my locker handle so I couldn't open it in the morning. My bully would throw food at me if I dared to order my lunch in the cafeteria. My bully repeatedly threatened to "rip off the wig" and laugh with others. My bully would chase me home from school with other kids until I reached my doorstep, then yell names outside my door. I was anxious almost every minute of class because I knew what was waiting for me when the bell rang. I would look out the window and feel like I was caged in. I felt like I was in this cage created by a bully, and the only one with the keys to let me out was him. When I saw the birds flying around, I always thought, *"I wish I was free like them."*

One day, it was lunchtime, and the sun was shining, so we were told to go outside for recess. A young boy who didn't typically talk much approached me. My bully was standing behind him. I stared into his eyes, and I could tell just from the look in them that he was going to do something or say something that he didn't want to do. I could tell by my bully standing firmly behind him that the young boy was most likely being peer pressured into this. The young boy said, *"take off your wig."* My eyes were welded with tears from embarrassment. He yelled this time, *"take off your wig, or I'll rip it off!"* Other classmates of mine started circling around him.

I could feel this huge weight all over my body, like my feet were stuck to the ground, and I couldn't move or think. I just stood there with tears rolling down my face. I looked around at each of my classmate's faces. None of them was smiling, but also none of them was speaking. I'll never forget the silence from them that day. No one said anything, and certainly, no one stood up for me. It was then that I realized it was up to me to stand up for myself.

At that moment, I decided enough was enough. I decided that I would no longer be the little girl in the blue hat or the girl who gets bullied for wearing a wig. I was no longer going to be chased home from school. I would no longer feel the gum between my fingers on my locker. I was no longer going to be called names or yelled at. I was no longer going to have food thrown at my face. I was no longer going to look at my feet when I was asked, "are you wearing a wig?" I thought, *"you can try to push me down, but still, I'll rise."*

I lifted my chin up, lifted my feet, heavy as bricks, off the ground, and walked toward the boy and my bully. My heart was racing, but I yelled, *"do it!"* And I bent my head over in front of everyone and pointed to my hair. I yelled again and got closer, *"do it!"* For a few moments, there was silence and no sounds except the birds chirping in the trees. They chirped so loudly, and I felt like I wasn't alone. Someone was cheering me on. I lifted my head and stared directly into the boy's and my bully's eyes. Neither of them said a word. By that time, a teacher walked over and asked what was happening. I said nothing, walked away, and proceeded back inside to class. The weight had lifted off my body, and I felt light when I walked. I felt free.

It turned out I had always had the keys to let myself out of my cage. You may ask, *"Sarah, where were the keys all along?"* Well, the keys were within me. The keys unlocked self-acceptance, self-love, and self-compassion. All I needed to do to find the keys was find myself. Sounds complicated, doesn't it? It isn't. The only step is to be authentically you; through being yourself, you will find your own set of keys and free yourself. Before you know it, you'll feel like those birds flying in the sky with your wings spread and sunshine on your face.

When I reflect on that eleven-year-old girl standing up for herself, I think about all of you. I think about so many other people going through something similar. Do you feel a heavy weight on you physically or mentally? Do you feel alone, like no one cares if you are alive or not? You're probably asking, *"How do I lift the weights, and how do I feel free and cared for like you do now?"* The answer is more straightforward than you think: stand up for yourself today and every day. Stand up for who you are and be authentically yourself.

Is it scary to stand up for yourself? Because you open yourself up to be hurt by others. But guess what? By not doing it, you'll be mentally hurting yourself. I know that from experience. Don't be blinded by how others think you should look or feel. You are all you need to be in this moment.

Just know that your light is already shining inside of you if you allow yourself to see. Love yourself when you aren't so kind, happy, or gracious and when you feel beautiful, loving, and friendly.

Through the bullying, I learned so much about who I am and who I am not. What stood out to me the most about my story is the lack of standing up for yourself and others. As children and adults, we can sometimes think *"silence is better,"* but in many cases, it is not. When I was being tormented daily, month after month, and year after year, I kept thinking, *"if I had a friend."* I would see all these girls who had a group of friends, and I would think that if I had some friends, even one, they would stand up for me, and my bully would back off. There were so many times when I would pretend to be someone I was not so I could gain a "friend" or "acceptance." But at the time, I didn't realize that I should never have to change who I am to have a friend, and if, in fact, they did become my "friend," it wouldn't be a real friendship. At the time, I never stopped and thought about what it would be like to be my own friend and fully accept myself. Accept yourself, love, and embrace yourself because when you do, the most amazing doors open for you.

I can proudly say that I am now the Beauty Editor for Bald Life Magazine. This position allows me to share my ideas on feeling beautiful with or without hair. I've had a photograph of myself published in the magazine completely bald, and wow, I've never felt more beautiful. I also created a group called Alopecia Makeup Tips on Facebook in 2019, which allows people to share tricks, tips, and advice on using makeup with no eyelashes, eyebrows, hair, or no hair. My group now has more than three thousand members in it. I use this platform on Facebook to spread light on Alopecia and support one another through the daily struggles. One of my proudest moments has been saying "yes" when asked if I would marry my now husband, Trevor. Through all the years of believing no one would stand up for me or love me for authentically being myself when I was ready to love me for me, I found Trevor. He has stood by my side for nine years, encouraged me to always be me, and shown me what love is like when someone loves you for all you are. When you love yourself, you allow others to love you as well.

Remember that your bad days are temporary and do not define you, but they are a part of your story. My childhood story is about beauty, sadness, happiness, strength, courage, and much more. Go out there and figure out what your story is, then look for the lessons in it, you'll find so many, and you'll grow so quickly. If you're having a hard day, month, or year, please say to yourself at the end or beginning of each day, "still, I'll rise" because you will, and you'll rise stronger than you were yesterday.

I Live the Bald Life!

Meet Sarah Cunha

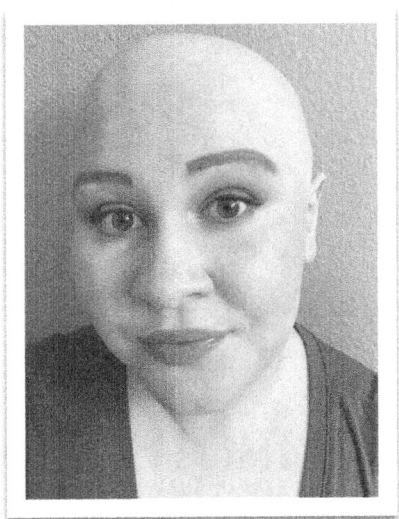

Sarah Cunha is a graduate of Quincy College in Massachusetts. She earned her associate degree in Psychology and is a contributing author and Beauty Editor for Bald Life Magazine.

She has spent years of her life advocating for people who are or have been bullied. Sarah created an anti-bullying website with her husband, Trevor Cunha, called Never Be Afraid to Stand Up.

Sarah is the founder of Alopecia Makeup Tips, a group on Facebook with over three thousand members. This group helps women with hair loss learn new ways to do their makeup.

Enjolé Johnson, Esq.

I dedicate my chapter to my younger self, all the young ladies that have lost their confidence and self-worth because of their hair loss, and Grandma Barbara, who loved me despite all my flaws… You taught me, unconditional love.

ALOPECIA DIDN'T BREAK ME

Women can do anything. We have proven that time and time and time again. –
Unknown

Imagine that you feel healthy, and everything is fine with your body. However, one day while touching your hair you feel no hair in the crown of your head. You're just a little concerned, but the patch grows over time. Now you're concern grows also. You begin to research to figure out what is going on and, finally, conclude that you have Alopecia.

Society glorifies looks and tells us daily that luscious hair is the standard of beauty we should all aspire to. So, having Alopecia made me feel different, like I did not belong. Having

Alopecia has been extremely difficult, physically, emotionally, and psychologically. Unfortunately, when people don't understand a specific issue, they minimize the impact the issue may have on one's life. In my case, I have been told many things, up to and including, *"at least you're not dying, I could never pull that look off, you have the head for that, and so many other things"*. Honestly, I know people are trying to be endearing and make me feel better, but actually, their comments make me feel worse. In addition to my hair loss, I wore braces and glasses. *Oh, what a trifecta.*

When I was younger, I had a nice full head of hair. I remember my mother would wash our hair (my twin sister and I) every other Saturday. After she blew out our hair, it would stand tall on top of our heads. I always used to think we were like Marge Simpson. My mother would plait our hair every day before school. And when there was a special occasion, we would get our hair pressed. What young black girl doesn't remember sitting in the kitchen with the hot comb, wincing and whining because she got burned? Who knew those would be the moments I'd look back on and treasure? My mother was adamant that I did not get a perm, but one day my twin sister and I came home with our hair permed. My mother was upset. I truly believe hair manipulation has had a huge impact on the state of my hair today.

Sometime in 7th grade, I had a scab on my scalp from getting a perm, and I was devastated, but I moved on like the issue would remedy itself, and it did. My hair grew back but little did I know it was the start of a cycle that would deplete my confidence and cause me to live in hiding for years to come. The next year went by without any issues. However, during my first year of high school, my hair fell out again. And I was devastated AGAIN! I did not know what to do. I cried and asked God, *"why is this happening to me?"* I knew there had to be a bigger purpose.

The first place I went to check, of course, was WebMD. That's right. As I researched, I realized I had the symptoms of Alopecia. WebMD told me I had every disease possible, and it really increased my concern. I walked around saying I had Alopecia. People ignored me and told me my hair was falling out because I did not take care of it. It was hurtful, but I also believed them because, honestly, as a young girl, I didn't know how to take care of my hair. I finally went to a dermatologist when I was about fifteen. After sitting in the clinic for hours, I was finally examined by a very nice, compassionate black male doctor. He was the first professional to confirm I had Alopecia. He handed me a piece of paper with the word Alopecia written on it and explained what it was, although I had already kind of known. I don't remember him recommending treatment; if he did, I did not follow up. A few months later, my hair was growing back on its own.

Side note - if you feel like you have symptoms, DO NOT self-diagnose. An early diagnosis can help limit hair loss. See a doctor.

Then I went to college. On my 18th birthday, I went to a hairdresser, and I remember her saying, *"Your roots are so thick, are you sure you do not want a perm."* I said, *"No."* I just wanted to dye my hair red. I was too cute. No one could tell me anything. One thing I've learned over the years is that when the roots of my hair become thick, dry, and brittle, my hair was about to fall out. That year was no different. In my first year of college, my hair fell out terribly. That's when I started wearing my hair in ponytails because it was easy and covered up the hole in the middle of my head. I did not realize I was literally destroying my hair with the ponytail because the pins would poke my scalp and split my hair as I placed them.

But then I got tired of covering my hair loss. I was bold enough to cut my hair. I still had a perm but did not love it. My hair was slowly growing back. I remember when an associate said I look better with longer hair. That hurt. One thing about me - I never really wore makeup and did not accessorize. Honestly, it was too much work, and I am far from high maintenance. At some point in college, I decided no more perms or manipulating my hair. I would go natural. I remember my friends would see my natural hair and say, *"Oh, your hair isn't that short."* But that was only because it was in a growth spurt.

I knew it would fall out again, and of course, it did. I began to accept that my hair would fall out every couple of years. It had become routine; I would touch my scalp and feel pain and a sensation. It hurt, but I could not resist touching it. It was weird. The pain and sensation still happen today when my hair is about to fall out. Usually, my hair falls out at the beginning of fall and/or the beginning of spring. As the seasons change, so does my hair.

Growing up, I did not go to salons often. The few times I did, I was always embarrassed. One salon I went to when I was in college was a unisex salon. I was so uncomfortable. I just knew everyone in the salon was talking about me, especially when I left. In another salon, the stylist pointed out that I had three dime-shaped holes in different areas of my head. The stylist was like, *"what is wrong with your hair? You don't take care of it?*" I was so hurt and embarrassed. So, I limited going back to the hair salon. However, there was one stylist that would pray over my hair, which was comforting. Last year I went to a stylist again but only AFTER my friend informed the stylist of my condition.

After college, my hair fell out several times. I remember sitting on my bed just taking pictures of my hair. It was so brittle, especially around where I grew completely bald. Wigs became my thing. And for me, wigs were too expensive; especially when I was not making much money. I did not know how to care for or style them, but I made do. However, it seemed like no matter how much I watched YouTube videos, my wigs never looked as good. I often saw people staring at my wigs while they spoke to me. I was constantly afraid that a wig would fall off. On this journey, my confidence was taken away. I never felt pretty enough or good enough. One day when I was preparing for an event, I was told I had to wear a wig. That hurt. I was going to wear a wig anyway, but this request confirmed to me that I wasn't pretty enough without hair.

In law school my hair fell out again, so much so that there was absolutely no way I could hide it. I tried, but I got tired of always wearing a wig. I was so insecure. Imagine having imposter syndrome and then also having to be worried about your hair. It was the winter of my last year, and I did a trial advocacy program. I cut my hair in the dead of winter. One day I felt a pain in the front of my head, and I noticed a patch was beginning to form. My partner at the time took me to buy clippers and shaved my head. I was so grateful, and I felt like I had a partner that really loved me for me. My peers who did not look like me asked why I would do that in the dead of winter. I just said I needed a change. I was not too fond of it. I remember seeing a guy from college at the train station, and I just cringed throughout our whole conversation. I felt so ugly. I acted like it didn't bother me, but it did. People said things like, *"your hair was falling out because of stress"*, etc. I knew that was not the reason. Then Ayanna Pressley came out. I loved it because representation matters. That's when I went on Facebook and told my story.

During the pandemic, there was a panel of women speaking about Alopecia. I subsequently reached out to one of the panelists. It is probably what propelled me to accept my Alopecia. I found someone else that was going through the same thing as me. It felt good not to journey this thing alone. She and I decided that we wanted to create a forum, which we named NakedCrown, and we are so proud of it. We wanted to encourage people, especially black men, and women with Alopecia. We wanted to let them know that they are not on this journey alone. Finding community is the most important part of this journey. In September 2020, we decided to do a 30-day launch with only a few followers. It felt great to share that I had Alopecia, mainly with friends and family. I felt like I could be myself. Now everyone in my life knows, and it feels so freeing. It actually made me more confident. I wasn't worried anymore if anyone knew I had a wig on.

And here's a story of when my wig did fall off. It was my 30th birthday, and we went to a lounge to hang. I was having a great time and was pretty much the life of the party. I swung my head a little too hard and maybe too many times. My wig fell off so fast. I laughed about it then, and I can laugh about it now, but it was still pretty embarrassing. Glad it happened in a pretty dark place, and I knew no one but my family and friends. We bounced after that.

Another pivotal moment was when Will Smith slapped Chris Rock on live television. Of course, violence is never appropriate, but that event brought attention to Alopecia, if only for a moment. I believe, in the black community, we don't talk about hair loss enough, although many women of all ages suffer from it, and that's unfortunate. Society tells us our hair is our crown and glory. This is what men are attracted to, right? However, we must become comfortable in ourselves to know that our hair truly does not define us. What defines us is our inner beauty. And yes, that all sounds cliche, and it kinda is, but it's true.

Over the years, I have come to accept my condition, and I am much freer and happier. I still often wish my hair would grow. I have a twin sister, and her hair is down her back. I still wonder why that can't be my hair. People often ask me why I still wear wigs, and I say because *"that's where I am on my journey."* I am not at the stage where I feel comfortable without it. Even though I still wear wigs faithfully, I do know that hair is not what defines me.

Although I really want this to inspire other women, especially young ladies with Alopecia, I also want to charge others around those with Alopecia to support them and learn more about it. Alopecia may not kill us physically, but it truly strips us of our confidence and self-image. Today, I am proud that I can make an impact and hopefully reach young ladies who feel like they are alone, or no one understands. I understand. I understand the confusion, the hurt, and the frustration when it feels like no one cares or understands. I get it.

Know that you are not alone. A community of loving women are ready to help you on your journey. And remember, everyone's journey looks different. If you're not ready to rock your baldie, don't. In due time, you'll know. Not too long ago, I spoke with a high school teammate who said, *"I never knew you had Alopecia."* He called me strong. And I believe it. I am strong; I am beautiful, my presence matters, and I make a difference. And you are strong; you are beautiful, your presence matters, and you make a difference. Loving yourself first is so important. External validation is only an addition to the internal validation you should give yourself daily.

Having Alopecia has taught me:

- the importance of community
- that it may be difficult to share that you have Alopecia, but it may be the thing that propels you into your purpose or at least increases your confidence.
- that loving yourself first is so important.
- a new skill, cornrowing. Try to focus on what you are learning through this experience. There usually is something positive you learn, even when you are hurting.
- there are many forms of Alopecia: Alopecia Totalis, Alopecia Universalis, Alopecia Areata, Central Centrifugal Cicatricial Alopecia (CCCA), etc.

Tips for those suffering from Alopecia

- Make sure to get diagnosed. It can help to possibly limit hair loss. Get a second and third opinion if need be because people are often misdiagnosed.

- When wearing and styling wigs, YouTube is your best friend.

- Accessorizing and makeup can help you on this journey.

- Research to learn more and find community.

- Follow NakedCrown on Instagram.

I Live the Bald Life!

Meet Enjolé Johnson, Esq.

Enjolé Johnson, Esq. was born and raised in the Bronx, New York. She obtained her law degree from Benjamin N. Cardozo in New York City.

She is a solid partner of NakedCrown, which launched in the summer of 2020 on Instagram. NakedCrown is designed to enrich and encourage fellow Alopecians to embrace their natural and authentic beauty. NakedCrown has guests every month to discuss various topics relating to Alopecia.

Connect with Enjolé Johnson, Esq. on social media:
Instagram: https://www.instagram.com/nakedcrown2020/
E-mail: nakedcrown2020@gmail.com

Melissa Dogonniuck

I dedicate my story to the 16-year-old, convinced there could be no future with Alopecia. Surprise, she strongly recommends a proper bald head massage. Once you humble your ego, you and this Alopecia thing will be friends, and you'll find peace in gratitude. There are so many special people to meet along your journey that will leave a permanent impression. Audacious, altruistic, and a touch of crazy, even without hair, you can still light up a room. You are absolutely going to love her.

BORN TO STAND OUT

"Although the world is full of suffering, it is full also of the overcoming of it."

— Helen Keller

6.8 million people in the U.S. have been diagnosed with a hair loss condition known as Alopecia Areata. Individuals may choose to hide their bald patch going unreported, so the actual number may be higher.

Aww, the desire to be normal, less complicated, happier, like everyone else. As a child, I would wish I could be in that regular line with all the "normal" children. Many moons later, I reflect that normal was a perception, a standard, set by others, and I am grateful I was never confined to a label, because I was born to stand out. Being unique is one of the greatest gifts to embrace. To be yourself seems simple, but it can take great inner strength and resilience to expose your truth of self-love and stand in it. Change came when my perception of normal changed; I loved myself and created light from darkness.

"Hardships often prepare ordinary people for an extraordinary destiny."

— C.S. Lewis

I often think about the "before" of an incident—before the phone rang or before that one event happened that changed into the "forever after" that changed you. When I was nine years old, I ran around our neighborhood with friends in a small suburban town, enjoyed sleepovers, and protected my special-needs sister. I enjoyed the stress relief that dance, and acrobatics class provided, and my mom was the Girl Scout troop leader. This was my "before."

My disabled sister—the happiest person in any room—is a year older, but during delivery, she lost oxygen for an extended time and will be forever four years old. During our elementary years, she had severe kidney failure and was in and out of the children's hospital. The stress on my parents mounted, and many arguments later, they divorced. Around this chaotic time, my mom found three smooth, dime-sized, circle patches of my hair missing. This was an "after" moment—I would be forever different. We went to the pediatrician, who said, "It will grow back. It is caused by stress." That stress diagnosis as the cause of my hair falling out felt backwards, as I now felt way more anxiety than I ever did before! There was nothing to be done, so we ignored the patches, and, through various hairstyles, I successfully hid them. The hair grew back, and over the next seven years, I enjoyed my unruly, thick, and beautiful curly long hair.

When I was sixteen, I invited a boyfriend I was crazy about to have dinner on a back porch with my family. I can still vividly picture this "before" moment in my mind. I was so happy and present minded. During dinner, I had my hair tied back into a ponytail. He looked at me and asked why my hairline was receding so high behind my ear. In that second, emotions flooded my core as I reached to feel my hairline and touched that smooth skin. I remembered that feeling. "It can't be," I thought. I jumped up from the table to run to a mirror to get a better look as my heart throbbed, and my eyes flooded with tears. Could this really be happening again? I didn't feel stressed out. In fact, things were going great. Nothing made sense.

Over the next six short weeks, as a sophomore in high school, my life changed forever. For the first time I was diagnosed with Alopecia Areata. I quickly became educated by two trusted medical providers that this was an autoimmune disorder and not a result of stress. Stress certainly can trigger a bald patch, but Alopecia is always with you, like an allergy. This condition has no cure, but there are experimental treatments that have had varying results, for example, getting cortisone shots injected into the scalp. One specialist advised me to buy a wig to prepare for the worst as there was no way of knowing its extent or duration. Alopecia Areata has three common forms:

1. Areata - leaves you with random patches of missing hair of varying sizes

2. Totalis - is total hair loss on the scalp

3. Universalis - is total hair loss on the entire body

Guess which form my competitive body went after for a really good challenge to my spirit over 6 short weeks? You guessed it!

Have you ever felt lost in a virtual hallway between two doors? The old familiar door is locked, and who knows what the door in front of you has behind it, but you are pretty sure you do not want to go in. I did not want to move on, accept this reality or buy a wig to hide it. It was all too much for my sixteen-year-old brain to process. I wanted to stay in that hallway, curl up in a ball, turn off the lights, ignore it, and wait for it to blow over.

Of course, life is about moving forward, so staying in the hallway was not a good plan. I bargained with myself. I knew my hair would grow back in time as it did before, so I tried to stay there. I tried everything to get my hair to grow back quickly. Those twenty-five cortisone shots directly into the bald patch on my head made perfect sense to me. The goal was for the steroid to reverse the body attacking the hair follicle. Yes, it was painful, but I was so numb that I would try anything. Oddly, at times, the shots felt strangely good. I was trying to stay positive, stress-free, and confident this would stop my body from rejecting my own hair. I just needed to endure, and it would get better. After a few sessions spaced apart, the doctor told me the hair was falling out quicker than she could safely give the shots, and we needed to stop until my body came to a stable period.

After a few weeks, I lost more than 25% of my hair. The mirror was changing so quickly that it was hard to keep up. My own body was attacking itself, and no one could help me. Time was not making it better; it was getting worse. My brain was so confused and sad, and nothing seemed to make sense. This is clinical depression. I told myself this could not be real as I locked myself away in my room. I felt genuine anger—such hatred. I would scream into my pillow and shake from my core as my throat felt the pain of constant choking from crying. I hated my appearance. I was a monster who should be alone and isolated.

Grief and emotional trauma feel like a nightmare with your eyes open. It is a constant state of distress and uncertainty. I had to relive the reality of my suffering each morning as my hair literally broke off at the scalp and fell off on well, everything. Preparing for school filled me with shame, sadness, and increasing grief. I am typically a tough girl, more humorous than emotional, but this condition was peeling away that confident self-esteem daily—the alarm sounds, I open my eyes and feel long strands of my hair covering my pillow. My heart sinks as overnight the friction of movement over my soft pillow broke more hair off the scalp.

I went to sleep crying, and I woke up crying. I could not wet my hair, or it would make the scalp too soft to brush. I could not detangle the hair when dry, or it would just pull the entire knot of hair out of the scalp. My heart ached as I cleaned out the hair clogging the bristles of the brush. I dreaded taking a shower. I would simply stand there, tears flowing, unable to catch my breath from the emotional pain of watching the hair fall down my body and clog the drain. My pillow, clothes, brush, and floor all needed to be cleaned through tears of grief before I somehow made it to the bus stop. I was organized, an honor student, and strong-willed, but now I could barely pull myself together. I felt numb, hurting. As each day passed, the more alone I felt, the more clouded my brain was, and I became a shell of who I used to be.

My mom thought it would be a good idea for me to attend an Alopecia support group meeting. I remember sitting in the very back of the room and listening with my arms folded to this group of people talk about their loss as if it was a positive thing. Some lost all their body hair, and that was hard to comprehend ever happening to me. "My hair will grow back as it did when I was nine," I thought. I refused to feel a connection with the group. I only saw what my brain wanted to see, the differences. They were all way older than I was, so they could not possibly understand being a teenager losing hair. I felt terrible for them and their stories, but I was not going to lose all my hair. They were not like me, and they were not my people. I did not ask to have Alopecia. I did not want to be part of this club. I left the meeting feeling like it did not help me feel better.

After several weeks into my mentally torturous morning routine, something had to be done about school. I was an excellent student and had lost all interest in attending school, studying, and taking tests. It all felt pointless. I could not ignore the fact that I could no longer cover the hair loss with various hairstyles, and about half my hair was gone. I decided to start wearing a hat if I was forced to go to school. Students were not allowed to wear hats, so we spoke to the school counselor and nurse, and they agreed to inform my teachers to make this exception effective immediately.

The next day, I arrived at school with a baseball hat, thinking this would help bridge the gap while I waited for the hair to grow back. Several students approached me, asking why I was wearing the hat. I just wanted to be left alone. I remember having difficulty remembering simple things such as my locker code, even though I had been using it several times a day all year. I remember feeling incredibly frustrated that my brain could not focus. I remember one day, sitting on the floor in the hallway, not feeling mentally well. I could not remember what class I was supposed to be in, where it was, or the bell schedule. It felt like I was in a thick fog of sadness. I finally pulled myself together long enough to remember I had a printed schedule and arrived at class late. As I walked in, the students were looking, and the teacher told me to remove the hat. I quietly said, "I have permission from the nurse to wear it."

He said, "Remove it or go to the principal's office." I left the room. Not feeling right, I went to the guidance crisis counselor and arrived in tears. I was told to come back because she was booked. Who turns away a crying teen at a crisis center? It was supposed to be a safe place to go for help. I felt so many had failed me at that moment. I told myself no one would be able to help me anyway. No one understands.

I wanted it all to STOP!

I went home feeling very alone. I knew my family loved me and wanted to help, but they could not. All signs were pointing toward total baldness with no eyelashes or brows. I did not want to live that way. It is not who I am. I could never accept this as who I will be. I questioned God. I asked what I could have done to deserve this emotional pain. I could not breathe. There was no hope; I could not imagine a future where this would be okay. My own brain told me horrible things. I locked my bedroom door. I attempted suicide.

My stepfather busted open my door. I was rushed to the ER and spent time away being watched and attending therapy sessions. I did not feel like I was worth saving, but luckily the good Lord saved me anyway as I had much still to do. At my first therapy session, as any teen might, I challenged the newly assigned therapist asking him if he had even heard of Alopecia. He said no. I said, "How are you going to help me?" By the next visit, he was better informed, and I became more open. Honestly, the sessions ended up being really helpful in guiding me to stay focused on what mattered. My stepfather helped me shave the rest of my head, so I did not need to go through the daily routine that was a smack to the ego. I was homeschooled for the remainder of the year. Within six weeks I was fully bald. I was sixteen with no body hair, head to toe, including eyelashes and eyebrows. It was Alopecia Universalis. I have been this way for thirty years.

The Shift Happened

Did you know, the National Institute of Mental Health has found that Alopecia Areata has been linked to depression, sadness, anxiety, and other mental health challenges?

The following September, I returned, finished high school wearing a wig, and joined the volleyball team as a setter. I enjoyed taking ownership of my own happiness and perspective. I remember trying a cheap dark brown synthetic wig and was near heat that literally melted my bangs, but I was in a group setting where no one said anything. When I realized this, I did not break. In fact, I found it hilarious. I was starting to feel like I had some choices and more like me again.

In my first year of college, I decided to go without hair and be bald. I attended Alopecia support meetings when I could, which helped with tips for handling stares in public without wanting to be verbally aggressive in defense. It was all an adjustment through small steps forward.

> "I can be changed by what happens to me. But I refuse to be reduced by it." — Maya Angelu

When I joined the workforce in my early twenties, I had my fill of being "her" when I entered a room. I needed more time to heal with privacy as I came to an acceptance of life with Alopecia. I remember trying to cover my crown during the day to not focus on it each moment, to give my brain a rest. I wanted to be more than my Alopecia. With a wig in public, I had more control over my healing and sharing my personal business. When I did choose to go out without hair, I carried homemade business cards with the definition of Alopecia to hand out to educate those looking at me, instead of feeling defensive. Success is incremental, so I treat myself kindly by appreciating each step forward.

I got married, had a baby, and my new life became my focus. Each summer, my husband and I would attend a conference in a new city for Alopecia. I submitted an article to the National Alopecia Areata Foundation, and my story, My Monster, was published in their newsletter. In addition, my husband and I ran a couple's session at one of the Alopecia conferences. I shared my humor about not having to shave, how sexy and soft our skin is all over, and wig mishaps. What I thought would end me was actually falling into place. Wait, who is this girl, joking and enjoying the benefits of a condition that left her entirely without hair, head to toe?

Lessons Learned and the Rise to Self-Acceptance

Alopecia has provided me with so many blessings. The rise to self-acceptance has no perfect formula, and everyone goes at their own pace, so I can just share what worked for me. I believe the journey to acceptance is all about perspective. You simply cannot fix normal so give yourself a break if you miss your hair and grieve what you have lost. It is a growing process that happens on your own time. However, I can share, as can many others, that the other side, is pretty friggin' amazing! So, try not to romance the loss as it will only keep you stuck. If you expect too much from Alopecia and its own timeline, you will be left disappointed, so control what you can. Patches, a wig, or no head accessory, go be you on your terms.

Connecting with other Alopecians is healthy and good for the soul. Find a meeting in your area, connect on social media, or start your own group as a way of giving back. I recently created my own blog and social media pages called Crowned with Alopecia to help others not feel as alone as I did. I write this today to help you see there can be light from the darkness.

Grief has five stages: denial, anger, bargaining, depression, and acceptance. I learned so many lessons, including resilience, through having Alopecia, and it has molded me into a better human. I recommend taking time for yourself with walks, reading, and writing your journey. Find clarity and comfort in your own mind. Speak kindly to yourself, and be patient, humble, and gracious. Focus on things and people you are thankful for, and perhaps write a message to a few of them. Fill your mind with positive things to remove the negative. Seek incredible speakers online, podcasts, or blogs for self-growth. If you like music, create a song playlist of favorites to find peace. Surround yourself with positive do-ers that make you feel empowered to step forward. For me, growth came from times when I was most uncomfortable, so do not be afraid to try something new. Pretty soon, you will look back and see how far you have come. Reach for the ceiling and make it a floor.

Once you move toward acceptance, your world will open up. Blessings and peace come from changing your perception of the situation. Happiness comes with hard work and self-reflection. It takes courage to step in a direction believing something good will be gained. Carve your own path and move in the direction of your peace. You will pick up knowledge along the way, adjust, and find your happiness. Love yourself and others. Alopecia is a superpower that lets our light shine and makes us magically different. If you embrace that, then there is no stopping the blessings coming to you and others standing in your light.

People do not determine your value—you do. If you are lucky enough to be different, courageous to show your unique self, and strong enough to carve your own path, do not change that or apologize for it. Stand with the courage to say, "Here I am, as I am" in whatever form of you makes your heart smile.

> *"We must be willing to let go of the life we planned so as to have the life that is waiting for us."*
> *— Joesph Campbell*

I Live the Bald Life!

Meet Melissa Dogonniuck

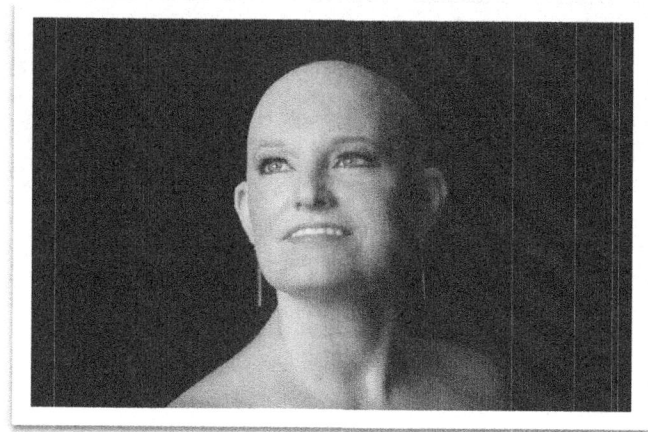

Melissa Dogonniuck is a successful Project Management Professional (PMP) for a large health system in the Philadelphia region and has worked in healthcare for more than 25 years. She successfully served a two-year term as chair of a colleague engagement committee to support her coworkers, organize events, and promote staff recognition.

She is an avid volunteer within her suburban Philadelphia community. With and without hair, she has a long-standing passion for charity and community service. She has organized countless drives to feed, clothe, and support those in need.

As a former Delaware Valley area Alopecia Areata support group leader, Melissa remains very active as a support advocate online, within forums, and in chats. Her dedication to the Alopecia community led her to start her website to help other Alopecians and their families find support at www.CrownedWithAlopecia.com. Melissa published her story in the National Alopecia Areata Foundation (NAAF) newsletter and has attended nationwide conferences.

In October 2022, she became a proud living kidney donor through Baystate Medical Center's transplant program in Springfield, MA. The recipient and his family are enjoying extra moments together, free from a dialysis machine, and Melissa feels like the lucky one to be able to share her spare kidney to save a life.

In her free time, Melissa loves hiking, reading, dancing, traveling, and soaking up moments with her family. She wears hair mostly in her professional life but admits being free to go without is the best feeling. She always says, "I was born to stand out."

Connect with Melissa:

Website: https://www.crownedwithalopecia.com/

Email: crownedwithalopecia@gmail.com

Photography Credit: Rebecca Barger Photography

Website: https://rebeccabarger.com/

Make-up Artist: Nicolette Brycki

Website: www.chiccosmetique.com

Makeda James, MPH

REDEFINING THE ESSENCE OF MY BEAUTY

"Challenges make you discover things about yourself that you never really knew." —
Cicely Tyson

Gasp and a long pause are never something you want to hear while your hair stylist is standing over you with your head in the sink and eyes blurred by fluorescent lights. Yet there I was, in August 2015, curious as to why Ms. Mea was gasping and at a loss for words. As she kept styling my hair, I could tell something just wasn't right. You see, Ms. Mae has been caring for my hair since I was in the 8th grade. She was responsible for my fabulous hair care and styles for over a decade.

I grew up being taught that my hair is my crown and glory. Or, as my grandmother so eloquently put it, "Ms. Kade, your hair is your beauty. Take care of it." From a young age, my beauty was wrapped up in what my hair did or didn't look like: how long it was, how healthy it was, and most importantly, how stylish it was.

However, on this day, when Ms. Mae turned me around in the chair, my beauty (or so I thought) was gone. Speechless, shocked, angry, and confused just to name a few emotions -I felt every low vibrational feeling possible, all at once. As the flood of tears and questions started, all I kept hearing was Ms. Mae's "I don't know what happened". You see, at that time, I was rocking my natural hair with the occasional side piece sewed in. My service that day was a simple wash and bantu knot twist out style. This style was one of the most basic for a naturalista like me. This is why I was shocked and confused as to why 70% of my hair was down the drain, and I was left looking like the "Cynthia" doll from the Rugrats!

The sadness on my face was immeasurable. I remember immediately going to my friend's house, seeking solace, trying to make sense of what happened, and trying to figure out how to fix it. The two of us were in the backyard, trying to troubleshoot and process what was going on and, more importantly, figure out what I was going to tell my mother. How was I going to explain this to friends and co-workers? How was I going to manage the barrage of questions that was headed my way?

I was not ready! I really wasn't ready. "OMG, I have to go to work! How am I going to do this?" was on a continuous loop in my head. I wasn't ready to explain over and over and over what happened or what was happening. Not only because I was embarrassed about how I looked, but I was also angry because I did not know who or what to blame. In an effort to take accountability, I asked myself over and over again, "What did I do to cause this?" Was it the result of too many perms, one too many color treatments, or was God punishing me?

After a few weeks of self-loathing and hiding under the $40 Beauty Supply store wig, I finally had an appointment with a dermatologist. This dermatologist came highly recommended by my mom, who, by the way, was just as perplexed as I was about my sudden hair loss. I decided to put my trust in her to find out what was going on. Bear in mind that every day leading up to the initial visit, I was in denial. You see, not too long before, I had surgery and started a new vitamin regimen to make my hair thicker. So, naturally, I blamed the vitamins and did not give any thought to the possibility of having Alopecia. After all, Alopecia only happened to women who did not take heed to the warnings of having their hair braided too often and too tight. "And I am natural, so there is no way this can be Alopecia".

Well, needless to say, I was completely wrong and was going bald as confirmed by the biopsy validating the doctor's initial diagnosis. As she tried to educate me on my diagnosis, a part of me blocked out any language about my hair not growing back and became solutions focused. I left her office with a bag of creams, scripts, and a prayer. After months of a variety of wigs and creams, I began to notice "Growth"! YASSSSS, I screamed in the mirror one morning as I noticed a few soft, brand new, baby hairs sprouting up across the front of my head. Sheer excitement coursed through my veins as I grabbed the phone to call my mom and share the great news. Up till this point, I was uncertain if anything I was doing was actually working. Those hairs, while small, light, and short, reassured me that "this too shall pass" and that I was well on my way back to a full head of hair.

"Look, doc! My hair is growing!! The treatments are working," I exclaimed as the doctor walked in. "Well, hold on, let me take a look." She responded. As I waited for her to join in my excitement, she sharply said, "Well, you know your hair is not going to grow back like Beyonce's." It was at that moment that I knew I was in the wrong place. I was insulted and confused as to why my hair growth wasn't being celebrated yet being minimalized by an unrealistic expectation that I didn't have. Little did she know, Beyonce wears wigs too! Hearing snide remarks from my health provider destroyed my spirit. Living with Alopecia was still a new space I was learning to navigate, and I needed every affirming word I could get.

As the months went on, my hair that grew back, soon after, it fell out again. There is a popular saying in the Alopecian community, "Hair in the Spring and Fall-out Fall," and I experienced just that. By the time I had my flare-up, I was emotionally over it. Losing my hair, I did a big chop and brought a new wig. However, in the Summer of 2017, I experienced a new level of Alopecia. "GOD, you snatched my brows and lashes!" I screamed as I was attempting to get ready for work one morning and noticed that my then-thinning eyebrows were now completely gone, and my lashes too! Yes, you read right, my lashes! Don't panic; they eventually grew back in.

Fast forward to my present life with Alopecia Areata. While my hair has not grown back since 2016, I have overcome several levels of self-acceptance. However, this did not happen overnight but in small incremental shifts over a period of time. It started happening when I stopped accommodating the considerations of others, redefined my personal definition of "beautiful," and remembered, I am still worthy. To date, I am still in the process of not allowing hair loss to define me (cue up I am not my hair by India Irie), as a learn to navigate new spaces without hair.

While there are so many other stories within my story I'd love to share, here are a few lessons I've learned along the way:

- You are still worthy of love whether you have hair or not
- You get to redefine the word "beautiful"
- You get to reinvent yourself anytime you please
- People don't care as much as you think they do
- Your hair is not the sum total of your beauty
- You're not the only one; find the others
- There is a resource for everything (brows and lashes included)

Self-love has very little to do with how you feel about your outer self. It's about accepting all of yourself."
— Tyra Banks

I Live the Bald Life!

Meet Makeda James, MPH

Makeda James, MPH is a public health professional and author of *"Relearning the Meaning of Beautiful!"* Born in the 80's to Jamaican parents, she earned her Bachelor of Science from Howard University in 2003 and pursued her master's degree at New York Medical College.

Beyond her professional duties - Makeda is an avid traveler, baker and former podcaster who loves being of service to her community through her sorority Delta Sigma Theta Sorority Incorporated.

Diagnosed with Alopecia as an adult, she struggled with hair loss for 5 years before sharing with others. Through sharing her story, she seeks to become a voice for the underrepresented and a source of inspiration to many.

Fall of 2020, Makeda finally decided it was time to share her Alopecia journey with others and seek out other Alopecians. This marked the beginning of the diagnosis becoming more personal, helping others. Out of a desire to help and meet others where they were emotionally, Naked Crown was birthed. The mission of Naked Crown is to enrich and encourage fellow Alopecians to embrace their natural and authentic beauty. Our vision is to provide a safe space for African American men and women with Alopecia to support one another on their journey as they become confident in their unmasked beauty.

Erika Hill, MCRP

I dedicate my chapter to my family, friends, and little Alopecians. To Monique Daniels, who listened to me cry on the phone. To my amazing dermatologist Dr. Osei-Tutu, for her compassion. To Dr. Zodelia Williams, for helping me find a barber to shave my head. To my siblings, Robyn and Eddie, for helping me with this writing process. Thank you, mom, for loving me through it all. To the little girl who has Alopecia, please know you are beautiful, you have power in your crown, and this autoimmune disorder does not define you.

FINDING JOY AFTER ALOPECIA

"Find Your Joy in Every Day"
– Erika Hill, MCRP

Have you ever wanted to snap your fingers and disappear mid-conversation? I have. In early 2019, my Caucasian co-worker handed me a few of my locs that had fallen under the office conference room table. Mortified, I froze wishing I was Casper the friendly ghost. I grabbed my fallen locs and rushed to my desk to put them away, while my unbothered co-worker brushed the incident off, because "his sister has this happen to her all of the time."

A mother's love is like no other but to receive love from another Black woman who treats you like a family member; dare I say a daughter - is an honor. Queen Owens, aka my childhood babysitter, was that woman in my life. I was her second daughter and as such, I have many fond memories of movies, shopping, her braiding my hair and playing go fish. When I became an adult, she was not just a second mother but a friend. Watching her decline and ultimately die of ovarian cancer was devastating.

Mental health and going to therapy have become trendy these days, however I started going to therapy back in 2014 following a rough break up. Maria Barnes, aka Dr. Bee, was the therapist who welcomed me, helped me heal and ultimately became a friend after our sessions were over. When I met her, she was bald due to chemotherapy, and I remember thinking how brave she was. She ultimately succumbed to cancer; however, I am forever grateful for her contributions to my life. Our last conversation was about how I was processing my dad's cancer progression. Losing her hurt and made me feel a little lost. Who would I call to unpack my feelings and emotions about things happening in my life?

Losing my father broke me for a while. I was daddy's little girl. We had daddy daughter dinners anytime my mother was away. He came home early to help me with my math homework. An electrician and plumber by trade, he taught me how to fix things. He loved to laugh, and we shared many inside jokes. I never imagined my dad leaving me before he walked me down the aisle at my wedding. I wasn't supposed to be saying goodbye to him before he could say hello to my first child. I lost a part of me the day he stopped breathing.

As the locs left my scalp, a little piece of me was lost

I had been a strong tree trunk; now, roots were coming up, and leaves were falling.

No spring flowers,

only April showers flowed from my eyes.

Sadness slipped in.

Grief grew.

Why was I losing people and things I loved? Queen, Dr, Bee, my dad, and my job.

Stuck and speechless, can I beat this?

So many questions…

Why is this happening to me?

What should I do?

Concealing my loss with smiles, scarves, and bobby pins.

"Fake it until you make it," they say, but I wonder, "did they mean until you make a decision?" Hmm

On a chilly morning on April 2, 2019, in Great Neck, NY, I sat waiting anxiously in the patient room with the remaining handful of locs barely attached to my scalp. The door opened, and in walked a melanin complected woman exuding compassion and understanding. Who was she? Dr. Osei Tutu, of Osei Tutu Dermatology. The moment she opened her mouth, I felt seen. I felt heard. I felt safe.

I had ideas about what I wanted to do with my hair if I could no longer have locs. I wanted a fro-hawk. Dr. Osei-Tutu said a baldie was the best option. I began to mourn the loss of my hair as I drove back to work. As the tears rolled down my face, I hoped that God, (who was getting me through the loss of my dad), would get me through this too.

Somehow, I was also motivated by my impending loss. In my car on that day, the Joy After Alopecia Journey was born. Alopecia Areata became my cause, and National Alopecia Areata Foundation (NAAF) became my initial source of connections. The project manager in me was activated, and I had things to execute. I couldn't see it at the time, but I was determined to find JOY. The key activities were finding a "safe place" to get my head shaved, getting my eyebrows threaded, and scheduling a photoshoot. Guess what? Putting those three activities into action, brought me JOY.

So, I became a baldie. However, the teenager in me who craved long hair was still inside me. Growing locs had been a huge accomplishment for me. I was finally able to have long hair without a weave or any added hair. Losing my locs, triggered childhood hair trauma from when damage from relaxers left me with unwanted short haircuts.

Even after shaving my locs, I was still keeping hair growth hope alive. So, I tried Janus Kinase, better known as JAK Inhibitors (pills that interfere with the immune system to prevent Alopecia Areata). Paired with high doses of vitamin d, and voilà, like magic, my hair was growing back. The extreme side effects of the medicine were awful. I struggled physically and cognitively. I didn't feel good, and I was forgetting and losing things like my apartment keys - in my apartment (I never found them, by the way).

The people pleaser and giver in me, felt I had to hang on for a full 30 days. Why? Because I had read in support groups that it was hard for others to access the medicine my insurance was covering for free. I also knew fellow Alopecians who really wanted to try this treatment but couldn't afford it. I felt I owed it to them. Stopping before 30 days would be letting them down. I legit felt guilty that I was even approved for the medicine and ultimately felt guilty when I stopped taking it. Thankfully, my loving support system, including Dr. Osei-Tutu, reassured me that I shouldn't continue suffering and shouldn't feel guilty. Once I stopped taking the pills, acceptance settled in, and I agreed to rock out with my baldie. The moment I made that decision, was when my true healing began, and my ability to find daily JOY came into view.

    Long brown fingers turned a page, the chapter read "New Beginnings."

    To truly begin a new one, you must unpack what you have been through.

    Invisible Band-Aids reveal unhealed wounds.

    As I ripped off the scabs, I faced the fact that I was still grieving my dad.

Through therapy and seasons of stillness, I learned the true impact of all the loss in my life. If I am honest, losing my hair triggered new grief about my dad. I longed for him to hug and hold me. I imagined him and me being "baldie twins." There was irony in that his battle with cancer resulted in hair growth for him, while his passing resulted in hair loss for me. I missed my dad. However, from sadness to stillness, the change did come. Do you suddenly want to sing *"A Change Is Gonna Come by Sam Cooke?"* I did as I wrote that last line, LOL.

Through stillness, I achieved growth.

I became less self-conscious and more self-aware of my emotional triggers.

I found natural (healthy) ways to cope when I became triggered.

I stopped letting my "loss" define me and what I was capable of.

I was reminded I am still worthy of love. I began actively practicing self-love.

I began vibrating higher and maintained it by being intentional about my food choices, staying hydrated, and practicing yoga and meditation. My new beginning meant new energy and the need for new practices. Because being by water brings me peace, I pursued a quest to find and visit waterfront parks in my immediate area and state. Even my first photoshoot while Bald was at a waterfront park. Whenever my vibrational energy gets low, I head to the beach or a waterfront park. I stand by the water. I practice yoga on the beach. I take cleansing breaths. Namaste. Inhale. Exhale. Child's Pose. Cue up, *"I am raising my vibration, yoga meditation (Vibrate Higher, Londelle)."*

Finding JOY after loss IS possible. It requires intention, commitment, and faith. I initially relied on my faith heavily to find joy each day. An easy one was that happy endorphins would be on fleek whenever I got a fresh Baldie. I would get my eyebrows threaded. Throw on some big gold hoop earrings and lip gloss, and I was "feeling myself." I took selfies, and I smiled from ear to ear. A fresh Baldie reinforced a positive memory of my first Baldie in April 2019. I playback the video of that experience a few times a year.

The more I poured into myself, the more I realized how much I loved about myself. My Joy After Alopecia Journey added another layer and hairstyle to my "Hair-Love-Story. I have been one of "Jerri's kids" towel please, called a Rasta and mistaken for a "him." The latter was one of my biggest fears. I kept thinking, "I can never step outside without wearing earrings or someone will think I am a little boy." Not enough people are "present." I am standing in front of you, fresh baldie, earrings, yet you still say he. Make it make sense.

Comments like: "I never dated a Black Chic", "At least you have a nice round apple head", "Do you have Cancer?", "Why did you shave your hair?", "I just want to lick your head", "Excuse me sir", and "Sorry man I didn't see you" while all still unwelcomed, have finally lost some of their sting.

I am NOT a HE, actually a SHE. I am HER. Strong, Bald, Black, Queen. I confidently rock my crown. Call me Alopecian, Black Queen, Sis. Please don't call me "him" and don't objectify me using my head. Forgive me if I am not excited by the backhanded compliments. Words matter, time heals, and self-love prevails.

As I stood still and focused on the moment, my senses were activated.

I could see. I could hear. I could smell. I feel.

Visuals of light blue skies.

Oxygen-filled lungs and solid heartbeat.

I feel alive.

Fall breeze hits my face sending a cooling sensation through my body, ending with my toes.

Feet firmly planted; I am grounded.

I have found that the little things bring me joy. There is merit in re-exploring childhood activities. I loved coloring books as a kid. During the pandemic, I bought an adult coloring book, and coloring those pages brought me so much happiness. Music has also bought me a ton of pleasure. I love listening to it, dancing to it, and singing along. In fact, in 2020, I took vocal lessons and performed "Nobody's Supposed to Be Here" by Deborah Cox as part of a virtual tribute to my dad. It still cracks me up how much he loved that song.

What else brings me JOY?

- Working Out
- Spending time with my family
- Mentoring black and brown youth
- Cooking homemade tacos

- Getting açai bowls from local black-owned business Swirl Bliss

Lesson #1: Loss happens in many ways and can be recovered from.

Lesson #2: After GOD, your relationship with yourself is the next most important.

Lesson #3: Finding ways to celebrate good times connected to the person or thing you lost can bring you joy.

Lesson #4. Remain open-minded to where you can find joy.

Lesson #5: Never apologize for how you feel.

Lesson #6: There is power in being present.

Lesson #7: Self-Love is imperative because life is hard

Lesson #8: Faith without works is dead. It is a team sport.

Let's talk about my faith for a minute. I have always felt blessed. I believed I have been fortunate. I prayed so hard for my dad to be healed. And he was but just not here on earth. My faith continues to guide me.

How can I believe in things I cannot see? With every new loss, I can't help but ask why is this happening to me? From friends to family, loss is inevitable. "Got to have faith, got to have faith, faith, faith." I believed I could, so I did. I had faith that I could, so I can. I manifested it, it will happen, so it is so. I am walking by faith, not by sight. My prayers will be answered. My increase is around the corner. My heart is joy-filled. My faith fueled me to find JOY.

Lord, order my steps.

Give me wisdom, strength, and guidance.

Grant me discernment for interactions I may have

in person and virtually.

Release me from the spirits of anxiety and fear.

I am a child of God.

I can do all things through Christ who strengthens me.

"All things" means you can shave your head, get a custom wig, fight that terminal disease, apply for a promotion, start a business, buy a home and earn more money. It starts in your mind and moves to your mouth (words have power). Whatever challenge or big decision you have to make, employ PMJT: Pray about it. Meditate on it. Journal how it will be once it happens. Take Action.

These single streets aren't loyal. I am searching for real love. Someone to set my heart free. My real love is a self-aware, healed Black Man with healthy boundaries. He will find my bald head beautiful and feed my spirit with peaceful affirming energy. Stay tuned for my love story. Until it unfolds, I will continue to love myself, love life and walk by faith.

"If you carry joy in your heart, you can heal any moment." Carlos Santana

I Live the Bald Life!

Meet Erika Hill, MCRP

Erika Elizabeth Hill, MCRP is a poet, social justice advocate, social entrepreneur, blogger, and author of the Alopecia Anthology Chapter, "Finding Joy After Alopecia." A professionally trained researcher and project manager, Erika has spent over a decade writing poetry and performing poetry that educates, inspires, and incites actions.

She is an award-winning CEO of her social enterprise, Vision Street Research LLC (VSR). VSR works with Black-led small to mid-size businesses and Black-led community-based organizations, providing project management, workforce development training, and market research & data analysis.

Erika's business seeks to provide research that impacts communities and creates access and opportunities for Black and brown youth in economically challenged communities.

She is a proud alumnus of The Edward J. Bloustein School of Planning and Policy at Rutgers University, where she earned a Master's in City and Regional Planning, and of HBCU Clark Atlanta University, where she earned a Bachelor of Arts in Business Administration.

In her spare time, she enjoys playing tennis, running, and mentoring young Black girls about self-care, self-love, and confidence.

Connect with her on social media @JoyAfterAlopecia & @VisionstreetResNY

Email: JoyAfterAlopecia@gmail.com & info@visionstreetresearch.com, Website: www.JoyAfterAlopecia.com & www.visionstreetresearch.com

Angela McCullers

I dedicate this story to my late sister, Kendra Lynette Young.

My sister was my best friend and the most loving person I've ever known. She was so strong and fought so hard throughout her cancer battle and she never complained. I'm so thankful that I was able to spend those last days with her. I learned so much about grace and mercy being with her during that time. She was simply amazing, and I miss her so much.

I would also like to dedicate my story to Jamie Elmore. Jamie, I know I was your problem child during this project, and I am so sorry. Thank you for not giving up on me. As I sat here in tears typing this, I realized that I was having problems moving on without my sister. I've been stuck and you gave me the push I needed to do something I always dreamed of doing. Thank you, my sister.

And last but not least my husband, Sylvester "Butch" McCullers, I thank you for always supporting me and being here for me through it all. I know I'm not the easiest person to live with but for some reason you love me and put up with my craziness. I love you!

HAIR LOSS IS NOT A DEATH SENTENCE

"Focus on What Matters Most – YOU!"

~ Angela McCullers

In 2009 I started getting an odd set of pains and symptoms that scared me because I hadn't experienced anything like it before. I was fatigued and in pain all the time. I had a loss of appetite, and because I didn't eat for a long time, I lost a lot of weight. Also, my mind was racing all the time, and I couldn't sleep or concentrate. I used to be an avid reader. That was my passion. I read at least two to three books a week, every week. That was what I did; I just read. But I haven't read a book since 2009. And I still buy them because I want to be able to read them, but I can't cause I can't concentrate.

One of the symptoms was a weird headache that often caused me to be a little lightheaded. At the time, being employed by FedEx Express as a courier, I had to drive a lot. Although I had no clue what was wrong with me, I knew it wasn't safe for me to continue working in that position, feeling like this every day. Within a couple of months, I found a new position that didn't require me to drive.

After many, many visits to doctors, urgent care, and emergency rooms, I was finally diagnosed with fibromyalgia AND lupus. I was relieved to finally know what was wrong with me. However, I was also quite scared because the only information I had about lupus was that the only person I knew with this disease died from it at an early age.

To say I was stressed out would be an understatement. My doctor started me on medications that made me feel a lot better, but that didn't last long because I was getting new symptoms. I had some stuff going on with my skin and ended up at the dermatologist. He did two punch biopsies on one of my legs that never healed properly and left scars on my leg. Then I started losing my hair and had to go to the Dermatologist again. He wanted to do the same biopsies on my head, but I wasn't willing. So, there was no firm decision on what caused my hair loss. Was it the other medical issues or medications, or was it actually Alopecia? One of the medications I was on was a low dose of chemotherapy that could also cause hair loss. The dermatologist gave me some Rogaine to apply to my scalp and wanted to do some more testing, but with everything else that I had going on with my health, I was at a point where I didn't care about my hair. I was really fighting for my life. That's how I felt because I had so many symptoms and pain going on. I had to decide to put my hair loss on the back burner because it wasn't life-threatening. Because I kept getting a whole new group of symptoms, my doctor sent me to do more tests, and eventually, I tested positive for rheumatoid arthritis, another autoimmune disease.

Even though I have Alopecia, most of my story doesn't come from it. It comes from my autoimmune disorders. So, at the onset of the diagnosis, hair wasn't that important to me. I saw it from a different perspective. Maybe if I didn't have all of that going on, I would've felt differently than what I share in this story.

I first noticed that my dreadlocks were falling out when one day I went to get my hair done. Some were literally hanging on by a strand. Then I lost one another day, and I was like, "What is going on?" I checked my head and saw the spots. I knew it would come to cutting my hair because I had a coworker who had dreadlocks and was losing her hair. She continued to wear locs despite hair loss, and I always thought, "She looks so crazy. She just needs to just let 'em go". At first, I decided, "I can't cut my hair." I loved my locks, and it would hurt to lose them. It would hurt to cut the locks off that I had worked so hard on for 10-11 years. However, I didn't want to find myself in the exact same situation as my coworker and said, "I'm not waiting until I look like her. I'm letting my locs go."

I had my hair cut and left enough to try a short afro. Every day I was in front of the mirror for an hour before going to work, styling my hair to ensure the spots were covered. It was depressing. So, after some time, I said, "That's it, I'm going to the barber and just shave it all off." Oh, what a relief. I was actually surprised by how many people looked at me and said, "Oh, that looks good."

I didn't even realize it at the time, but I guess, subconsciously, I was missing my hair. I usually wore a cap and would sometimes let my hair grow to see if the spots were gone, but it appears they are with me for life. Sometimes my baldness bothers me, but I have to say I'm just happy that I have my life.

I remember the first time I could say I was truly happy that I was bald was when my sister, Kendra, was sick. She had rare cancer and went through all kinds of chemo, radiation, and surgeries. And when she lost her hair, it made it a whole lot easier for her. She was my biggest supporter when I cut my hair off. She was my cheerleader. She was there for me, and when she needed me most going through that all of what she endured, I told her, "Hey – your big sister's already bald," and cheered her right through it. So, it made it so much easier for her. We're just going to be bald together.

Although my sister never shared with me how much me being bald helped her, we both knew it did. I think the biggest thing was that she knew she wasn't alone. We made jokes about it. One time I was visiting my sister after she came home from the hospital after her surgery. Me, my brother, who lost his hair early, and my sister were in there when our mom came in. I looked at her and said, "Mom, I bet you never thought you had three baldheaded kids." And we all just died laughing. We would make jokes and roll with it. I think my baldness and jokes helped her a lot in her battle with cancer, from which she eventually died.

The best part is I never really got negative feedback about being bald, except for one person. When she saw me the first time, she said, "Why did you do that? Why didn't you get a weave?" I replied, "I don't want to wear a weave. The one time I remember getting braids with extensions, it lasted two days. I paid $200-$300 to have it done, and I couldn't take it. I pulled it all out."

I'd even bought a couple of wigs. I tried it for maybe a year. And I remember one of my aunts saying, "Oh, that looks so nice. That's how you should wear your hair." But I knew I was NOT going to keep wearing wigs either because if one of those hot flashes hit me, I'll pull it off even while sitting at church. I didn't care. I remember one night; I was getting dressed for a party my husband and I were going to. I put a wig on, thinking it would keep everybody from staring at me all night. However, when we were getting ready to leave, I kept looking in the mirror and finally said to myself, "This is not me anymore." I took the wig off and went to the party. And that's how I've been rolling ever since. I had gotten to the place where it doesn't even phase me anymore.

I remember this one girl called me a baldheaded b**ch. I looked at her and said, "Make sure you say that's a cute baldheaded b**ch. Okay?" and laughed. That was freedom.

At some point, I found support groups on Facebook. I never knew anything about Alopecia and never knew there were groups for it. But, after joining a couple of the groups, I felt at home. I didn't realize how much I needed something like that until I met all these ladies: Jamie Elmore and the rest of the sisters. Being a part of the support groups gives me a new outlook on it because I'm seeing what the other sisters went through. I guess the way they felt about losing their hair was kind of like how I felt going through the other autoimmune diseases and stuff. And I guess I really didn't allow myself to go there because I was busy dealing with the other issues and thought that was most serious at the time.

Lessons Learned:

Even though the hair loss didn't affect me the way it did others, some see it as a life sentence.

    I have a close girlfriend who had long, beautiful curly hair. She was diagnosed with breast cancer and lost her hair due to chemotherapy. She told me that losing her hair made her feel worse than when she got her cancer diagnosis. And that made me realize how serious it was for other people. I didn't know that to some people losing their hair was like losing a limb. I never felt like that. I grew up as a tomboy. I liked to look good but never thought that much about my hair. I kept it looking nice, but I would play basketball or softball and not care when it was a mess. I would just wash and curl it again as a regular part of grooming. I was always regular. I was never caught up in being a girly girl, but I know how to when I want.

    I would say you have to learn to love yourself and not be consumed with what other people think and what other people are doing. It's okay to be unique. It's okay to be an individual. You're not everybody else. You got your path, and it is not going to be everybody else's path. And this happened for a reason. Most importantly, Hair Loss is NOT a Death Sentence.

I have had people walk up to me and tell me I was beautiful and that they had hair loss as well, and they didn't have the nerve to come out like I did. And I hurried up and invited them to the Bald Boss Community, which is the Alopecia support group that I am now a member and a leader of. I said, "Come on to the group and talk to the members, see what everybody else is doing, and maybe you'll feel different cause you're not by yourself." I like helping people.

My neighbor has a granddaughter who has Alopecia. I didn't know. I was talking to the neighbor next door to them, and a little girl came out on the deck; she saw me and stared. Then she started smiling and waving. And I waved back and then walked over to their fence and started talking to her. I said, "I believe you have Alopecia." And she replied, "I do." She had never seen another woman with a bald head and was so excited. After talking to her, I called Jamie, who sent her a bald Barbie. The girl was so happy, smiling ear to ear, and that just made me feel so good.

Love yourself and know that you are not your hair. Always remember, hair loss is Not a death sentence!

I Live the Bald Life!

Meet Angela McCullers

I'm just a county girl from Goochland, Virginia. I currently live in Baltimore, Maryland with my husband, Butch. I recently retired from FedEx Express where I was a courier and a sr. service agent. I am on the leadership team of the Bald Boss Community, a support group for men, women and children living with Alopecia.

Connect with Angela on social media:

https://www.facebook.com/angela.y.mccullers

https://instagram.com/bmorebaldie

Chloe Bean

I dedicated my chapter to my parents, Bob and Lisa Bean, as well as my twin brother, Carter. I could go on for pages about how much you all have supported me through my Alopecia journey, and it would never be enough. When I was going through my lowest time, you all did anything you could to make me smile. From my mom and dad helping me shave my head, to my twin brother standing up for me when I was being bullied, my family always took care of me. I wouldn't be who I am today without the love and support from my family. ~ Chloe Bean

THE ALCHEMY OF LOVING YOURSELF

"To fall in love with yourself is the first secret to happiness." - Robert Morley

What would you do if one day you woke up and noticed your hair falling out? How would you feel seeing a core part of your image shift drastically?

    I had to overcome this challenge as a young girl – and I still face it daily. My name is Chloe Bean, and I've had Alopecia since I was eight. Having a condition that impacts my appearance resulted in a lifelong battle with plenty of ups and downs. It also taught me a lot. Each day I learn and grow more and find new ways to be empowered by my Alopecia. If you follow along to hear my story, I'm confident I can show you some of the lessons I've learned and help you turn your *"flaws"* into strengths.

No matter if you have Alopecia or other conditions that may cause hair loss, I believe my message can inspire and encourage you to stand strong. Even for those without hair loss, the message I have to share holds true: accepting and owning your perceived flaws and turning them into strength and light.

My journey with Alopecia has been my life's greatest struggle but also my greatest strength. I went from being "different," an outcast, having to wear hats in school, to sharing informational CDs about my condition with my classmates. I was called names and bullied. It got so bad I wanted to be homeschooled in high school. I generally did not feel happy, proud, or comfortable with my own self…

Then I transitioned into being a bright, shining light, accepting my condition, and owning it, letting it empower me (and others). And it was a challenging, painful process to get there. But in doing so, I was able to let my true power shine through and have been able to make an impact on thousands of people around the world.

When I was a little girl, I had long, dirty blonde hair that would engulf my entire back down to my waist. It would take me hours to brush through each tangled section and then style it to look presentable. I never complained about it. If anything, I absolutely loved having long hair.

Then I started waking up to find clumps of my hair scattered throughout my bed, and as time went by, more and more hair would just fall out for no reason. I had no clue what was happening to me.

What was going on? Why was I suddenly losing my hair?

My parents started noticing small bald patches in various sections encircling my scalp, many the size of a nickel or a quarter. It got to a point where my parents became so concerned, they took me to a doctor in hopes of seeking medical help.

After being sent to various hospitals, the doctors finally diagnosed me with Alopecia. I learned that Alopecia is an autoimmune disease that causes your immune system to attack your hair follicles, resulting in hair loss. I also discovered that I wasn't alone – approximately 2.5 million people in the United States are affected by Alopecia. And I did learn that Alopecia can be triggered by stress or other environmental conditions, but in my case, it was a genetic condition (and it wasn't likely to go away). My great-grandma on my mom's side happened to have Alopecia. So, it was hereditary. Everyone else in my big Italian family was hairy, but baldness was my reality. I felt like the black sheep of my family.

As a stress-free child, I was disturbed about how this could even be happening to me. I would often ask, "Why me, God?" or "Why do I have to be the person in my family with this?"

Over the years, life with Alopecia didn't get any better or easier. There were various times that I would look at myself in the mirror and break into tears from hating the image reflected in front of me. Every day I would wake up, the first thing I saw was my pillow covered in clumps of hair.

Even worse was not wanting to brush my hair because every time I did, I'd see strands of hair slowly fall to the ground. Hair is the most visible characteristic of the body and can be considered a core trait of femininity for women, which made me feel like I'd lost a part of my identity.

It started out as small patches, but then within a few months, I was almost bald. You can only imagine what I was going through at such a young age. All I wanted was to be considered a "normal" little girl with luscious locks of hair, but I couldn't have that. I could not come to terms with why this was happening to me. As the days passed, I dreaded going to school. But I still went with a hat on my head and a smile on my face each day of the week.

High School came along, and my bald spots went away. For two years of high school, I had long, thick, dark hair that ran down to my waist. Then, one day during my sophomore year, I saw more bald spots. I was crushed.

By junior year, I had such big bald spots that I couldn't cover them anymore. It was a horrible year for me. Living in a small town, I was mortified to be around everyone, and I wanted to just hide away from everything and be homeschooled.

I went to school every day wearing hats, thick headbands, wigs, and anything to cover up my bald spots. I felt like an imposter - like I wasn't myself. It was hard going home every day and having to take off my wig and confront the reality of my appearance. When my brother would have friends over, I'd go upstairs and put my wig on or simply hide in my room so nobody could see me.

Around that time was when I started to try wearing wigs more and gained confidence and perspective that changed my life. The wigs made me feel like "me" again. As I gained confidence, I started to see them more as a positive side of having Alopecia. I could switch up my style or color any day of the week and viewed wigs as an accessory, a way to make being bald fun and unique.

I started to see things from a new perspective. I began to realize that physical appearances are not what is most important in a person, and if somebody can't accept me bald, they are not worthy of my time. I also began to embrace that what was happening to me was ultimately out of my control.

The wigs were a win for me, but I still had to face what was in the mirror. Then there was a day when I found light in my situation and took control of my Alopecia. Instead of continuing to look in the mirror and hate what I saw, these huge bald spots, I decided to shave it all off.

Next thing I knew, I was completely bald - not a single strand of hair existed on my round, peanut-shaped head. I remember thinking there was no way I could ever come to school and walk down the halls with a smile on my face.

What did I do, though? I mustered up some courage and walked into the doors of my high school bald for the first time. I still remember to this day how vulnerable and inferior I felt. I could feel the burden of various eyeballs staring me down and following every step I would take. I had absolutely no self-confidence left within me. How could a bald teenage girl be accepted by her peers?

Most days, I would come home from high school teary-eyed, and other days I would have a mental breakdown. I soon became isolated from everyone around me. I would rarely leave my house or even my room.

But shaving my head was the first step to help me shift my perspective, and when I did that, everything changed.

Bouncing Back

"Stop comparing yourself to people. You're only on this planet to be you. So be you." - Unknown

Shaving my head was a pivotal moment for my story. Just as I'll never forget the day, I walked into my high school bald, I'll never forget when I first posted myself bald on social media. Coming from a small town in Midland, Michigan, it's hard to share something personal, and you know everyone will see it. The outpouring of support was an incredible help for me mentally and emotionally.

I found my community of people who had Alopecia or went through chemo and others who had other hair loss issues worldwide. They were all going through something, just like me. Finding that community gave me more strength than I could've ever imagined.

On top of finding my community, I found massive relief simply in embracing and facing my condition head-on. It felt like a huge weight had been lifted from my shoulders (no pun intended). It's so hard to take that first step whether it's going out in public bald, posting online, or even just telling your friends or family – but when you do, amazing things happen. You love yourself more, and you shine differently. These things always take time, courage, and effort, but trust me, it's worth it in the end.

I'm proud to be able to contribute to the community of people with hair loss like me, and what's more, I've found purpose in my condition. It fulfills me to know that I can inspire people going through the same things I have.

For a long time, I had been a victim of my condition. It was the worst thing to ever happen to me, and I viewed it as such. But once I started to accept what was happening, I took control of the condition rather than letting it control me. Instead of looking at my autoimmune disease as a setback in my life, I could see the positives.

I've now stopped questioning why this happened to me and can look at the brighter side of things. Having Alopecia allowed me to become a confident woman who always has an open mind. I am more empathetic and understanding of others. I am happier with myself as a person and less dependent on my appearance.

Hair may be considered a core trait of femininity for women, but not having hair allowed me to find true beauty. I am bald for a reason, and although it gets hard sometimes, I have a story to share and a purpose in this life to fulfill.

In the End

You can turn any weakness into your greatest strength with a different perspective.

But whatever it is, you have to face it head-on. The first step in overcoming any struggle is acceptance — if you deny it or try to run from it, you will inevitably face that struggle again. It won't simply go away.

With acceptance comes the open-mindedness necessary to shift your perspective. That simple shift in perspective is all it takes to see the positive in your situation and create something beautiful out of it.

I'm not saying acceptance is easy. It can take years to reach that point of acceptance (and often, it comes with the other stages of grief, such as denial, anger, etc.), but I promise that once you get there, good things will come.

Embracing my baldness and sharing it on social media has sprouted into much more today. I am proud to make content full-time that's focused on inspiring and empowering people to feel confident in their skin (wig or no wig) and bring awareness to Alopecia and hair loss. I own a brand that sells products for people with hair loss that I use daily, such as temporary eyebrow tattoos or wigs. These little products can go a long way in making you feel comfortable and beautiful.

<u>Tips for those facing hair loss</u>

- Take control of something you have no control over by accepting and facing it head-on, whether that be shaving your head, embracing your bald spots, or wearing wigs - whatever makes you happy.

- Have fun with it. Hair loss means you can be whoever you want to be, rock whatever look you want and have your own uniqueness.

- Give yourself time. Don't expect yourself to be completely comfortable with your hair loss right away. Let yourself process it, however, you need to - it's not a race.

- Don't lose faith in yourself. Hair loss is hard. Having faith and never losing hope is something I had to remind myself of constantly, but eventually, it will stick with you.

Whatever your flaw, weakness, or struggle is, whatever you hate about yourself, you can turn that into your greatest weapon. And when you do that, you'll not only respect yourself and love yourself more, but people will notice because you will have a different glow when you've gone through hell and come out stronger.

ALOPECIA: OUR STORIES

I Live the Bald Life!

Meet Chloe Bean

Chloe Bean is the founder of Baldie Bean Beauty, a business that offers eyebrow and hair products for people with hair loss. She is an admired content creator who inspires millions with her stories about overcoming hair loss.

An empowering creator who has helped people from all walks of life with hair loss, Chloe made her name by sharing her experience of going bald at eight years old. A loved social media influencer, she has been creating content for over three years, sharing tips and tricks on all things — hair loss — which led her to found her brand this year (Baldie Bean Beauty).

Chloe's content has received over 100 million views on TikTok and continues shattering social media records. Chloe is from Midland, Michigan, where she grew up in the snow and on a pair of skis, but now lives in Scottsdale, Arizona, where she loves to soak up the sun!

When she's not making content or working on her business, Chloe has worked with some amazing brands such as Summersalt swimwear, Philosophy skincare, and more.

Delena Thompson

I dedicate my chapter to my grandmother Rosie Bell. You were the pioneer of our family. You always made the impossible possible despite our lack of vision. Your love and strength carry us on today. I thank you for the lessons your unwavering love and support taught us. I thank you for the path you have created for us. Thank you for continuing to watch over us from heaven. May I continue to make your memory proud.

MY FIRST TIME AT THE WIG STORE

"Your past is a lesson... Not a life sentence"
~ Unknown

It was September 1980. After spending summer vacation with both my paternal grandmother in Albany, NY, and my aunt in California, it was time to return to school. Due to the sudden changes in my hair, I always wore a knit hat. The bald spots impacted my self-confidence, and I felt shame. My stomach would knot up with the fear of being questioned: "What's wrong with her?" "Why did she look like that?"

My maternal grandmother decided we were going to the wig store where she buys her wigs. We entered the store, and of course, everybody was looking at me. I could imagine them thinking, "Why is she here?" I cried the entire time. My grandmother's attempt to comfort me by saying, "Don't cry, Lena," did not help alleviate my shame and fears. The store owner, Mr. G., took me to the back so that I could try on a wig. However, the wig was too big, and my tears started to flow more. My grandmother bought the wig regardless and later made alterations so that it could better fit me.

My self-confidence was lacking; I had glasses, a square Afro wig, a skinny pencil shape body, and no eyebrows. I had such a hard time embracing myself that it made me scared to defend or speak up for myself.

I tried to defeat the internal battles I was facing, but I felt scared of being alone. I never really had friends just sister and a hand full of people that wanted me to be their friends. My grandmother would try to build up my self-esteem. I recall her and my mother enrolling me in a karate school. However, after going to karate school 2-3 days a week and learning to hit back, I still needed my little sister and family to stand up for me when I was being bullied.

I was later enrolled in Barbazon school of modeling, where I took makeup classes with the hopes it would help me love myself. Attending these classes, I learned how to draw on my eyebrows. This new skill boosted my self-esteem. In addition, I enrolled in fashion classes, where I learned how to walk with confidence and improve my sense of style.

A lot went in my brain from all the classes that I attended. However, the one thing I observed that stuck with me was the fact none of the other girls in the pageant wore wigs; I was the only one. Therefore, as time went on, I accepted the fact that the girl with the beautiful silk straight or curly hair and light-toned skin would win the pageant, which she did. I was happy for her since she was my friend. Despite not winning the pageant, I finished the class with honors and became a model for the School of Barbazon.

As I entered High School, I expected that becoming the young woman I knew I could become. I found it very difficult for me to learn. That was a side effect of having had lead poisoning. I continued to face bullying that tightened my stress level and impacted my ability to learn. My younger sister always acted as my bodyguard and always stood up for me. I found it funny that instead of me watching over my young sister, she watched over me.

While changing to go to physical Ed class, classmates would make fun of me, stating, "Your legs and arms have no hair because you're bald." They would laugh as I got dressed, fighting back the tears. I dreaded going to the gym or doing anything physically related.

I would pray my wig did not fall off when going on field trips. I always had to wear a swim cap while I was there. The kids would let their hair get wet and say things to me like, "Take the swim cap off before I pull it off." I would cry, knowing the kids would laugh because I was bald.

Although there were kids that wanted to be my friends, they were scared because of what other kids would think. So, I did not have friends and dealt with others laughing about me and whispering to others. My experiences in high school made me feel defeated. I could not change my appearance. The only thing I could do was to turn away, ignore the bullying and simply focus on my education. I gave up on the notion of making friends, being accepted, and being seen for who I was.

I don't know how others dealt with the same situation. I was traumatized by it. I can remember everything like it happened yesterday, forever recorded in my brain. All the things I dealt with were sickening and hurtful. Despite these scarring, life-changing experiences, I am thankful for everyone in my corner.

Alopecia is difficult for people to deal with as a child or adult. It was always hard embracing myself, but one thing was for sure, ugly ducklings can always turn into swans. I thank God for my grandmother during these hard times, for always keeping my head up and assuring me that one day, things would change.

Being a young Afro-American girl and growing up in the projects, it was hard to see myself as the beautiful, intelligent young lady I was. I am thankful to all the people who supported me and always looked out for me. My little sister was a big part of my life; she and my maternal grandmother were always my heroes. I love my family and friends for all the support. I learned not only who I am but also the valuable lesson that the people who really love you will stand by you through the bad, the ugly, the mess, and the good.

God has taught me to love myself because he loves me, and I am created in his image. My journey has taught me that the notion that a person isn't beautiful because she doesn't have hair, or her skin looks different is a lie. You're beautiful inside and out. Always remember that life is too short. Never judge a book by its cover. If you never know where you've been, you'll never know where you're going. Be grateful for who you are and what your purpose is.

I am blessed.

I Live the Bald Life!

Meet Delena Thompson

Delena Thompson was born in Albany, NY, in 1967. She is the first of three children. She noticed she was different when she had Alopecia as a little girl and had to spread the word that it was not a disease but a hair loss.

  Delena is a very humble and caring person. She always goes above and beyond to help others. She is a public speaker for Massasoit Community College. This book project is the second of her authorship. She is also the producer and star of the 2016 BNN Media Network of Boston documentary titled *"The Girl from Orchard Park with Alopecia Areata."*

Leonard & Sizakele Chaplin, MBA

We dedicate our chapter to all the couples and Alopecia warriors who had to experience Alopecia in their unions. We know and understand the emotional roller-coaster, struggles, and triumphs associated with living with the condition. And we want you to know, YOU ARE NOT ALONE. ~ Mr. & Mrs. Chaplin, MBA

IS LOVE REALLY BLIND?

"There is no difficulty that enough love will not conquer." Emmet Fox

Sizakele

Shortly after creating a profile on a Christian dating app, I met a person I really liked. We had been talking daily for just over a month and for hours on end, and I thought we were getting serious. I had even planned to move to his state, which was a six-hour flight from my location.

He didn't know about me having Alopecia because I wore a wig in all my pictures on my profile. I was not yet comfortable with the bald look. Answering a question about my hair type on the questionnaire section, I wrote "short". I don't think they had bald as an option for women. Or maybe they did, but I was not going to select that, was I. At that point, very few people knew I had Alopecia. I was so ashamed of my condition. About 60% of my hair was already gone. I wore accessories or wigs on my head everywhere. When I was diagnosed with Alopecia and had to face the reality that one day, I would be completely bald, I thought this would push my potential partners away. For me and for many other women, my hair was synonymous with my desirability and femininity. Even if someone knocked on my door, I would never allow anyone to see me without a covering on my head. I couldn't even look at myself in the mirror. I was in a bad place in terms of acceptance of my hair-loss condition. I also didn't know much about the condition. The only thing at the back of my mind was that I might not have hair for the rest of my life. It was very upsetting to even think about. But life had to go on, and if I wanted to get married one day, I had to go out there and be vulnerable in the dating world.

The plan was to be found by someone who would love me with all my flaws. A God-fearing, empathic, loving man who was not materialistic. I needed a man who would fall in love with my personality and not see my bald head as a weakness or lack of beauty. I wanted to be together because of who we are, not just because of what we look like.

I finally summoned my courage and asked my date if he knew what Alopecia was. He responded no, so I asked him to research it and come back to tell me what he thought about dating someone with that condition. I didn't say I had it. It turned out that love was not blind to him. He couldn't stand the possibility of dating someone without hair. He ended it without an explanation.

I think whatever he learned about Alopecia was not what he expected. His response made me feel so ugly, which confirmed the story I had been telling myself for over seven years since I was diagnosed – that I was unlovable and undesirable. Who would love a woman with no hair? I mean, most black women would do anything they possibly could to have "*good hair days.*" Women spend thousands of dollars just for wigs and hair treatments. Here I was, losing the very thing that I valued so much and that, as I thought, drew the attention of the other gender.

After being disappointed, I made a mental note to get deactivated from the dating app. I kept telling myself that it probably wasn't for me. It was an American thing, after all, and I am from South Africa. I still believed in a man approaching a woman the old-fashioned way: simply walking up to her at a town event or a church social or gym and saying a genuine hello, A naturally started conversation and the feeling of a little spark fly were much better in my point of view than meeting someone behind a screen and wondering if they are the one.

However, I decided not to cancel my pre-paid membership and took one month break instead. When I returned, I was ready to mingle again. The next person I met was a man with the profile name 'LJ'. We hit it off immediately and had so many things in common. I remember thinking, this could be my prince charming. I wondered if he would still be interested in dating me if he knew I had no hair on my head.

I was doing this levelheaded this time and was not going to allow my hair loss situation to derail my dating life. In fact, I was prepared to use this as an opportunity to fully embrace every part of myself. I was not going to make the mistake I made with the first guy. Before our first in-person date, I took the courage to tell 'LJ' my skeletons.

We probably talked back and forth for about two weeks daily for hours on end. We spent hours texting, and at this point, we were ready to exchange numbers. I had gained enough courage to ask him if he had any secrets, he wanted to share with me. Things that he was ashamed of, maybe things he had done in his youth and had regrets over. But not only that, I asked him to share things that he felt could affect our relationship. This could've been mental, physical, and even health issues.

LJ shared with me what ended his first marriage and that he was scared of committing to someone because he was afraid it might end in divorce again. People with issues also want to be loved. Wait, don't we all have some issues – just at different levels?

It was my turn to share my "secrets." I asked to call him for this one. I didn't want to type and wait for a thought-out or rehearsed response. I wanted to hear his immediate reaction when I told him. I was super nervous and anxious about his response, but it had to be done. It was now or forever hold my peace. Also, I was ready to use this conversation as a teaching moment should it not go the way I expected. Knowing his weaknesses and vulnerabilities I would be able to help him understand that a condition like Alopecia is not something you wake up and decide you want. It's an auto-immune condition that has forced me to lose my hair. If I had it any other way, I would choose to have my own hair again.

Leonard

We were about to go on our first face-to-face date, and I was looking forward to meeting Sizakele in person. I already knew that she was special. There was just something about her. She was the woman I had been praying for all these years. Our super-long telephone conversations - were all so refreshing. She had this spark about her, and her personality was just so warm and welcoming. Part of our conversations included some hard thought-provoking questions about our family histories and things I overlooked before getting married to my ex-wife. I was determined to do it right with Sizakele and anticipated sharing things I was uncomfortable with, including reasons for my divorce.

I am an ordained pastor and don't consider dating a joke. I joined the dating site with a wife in mind. I was not prepared to play games or make the same mistakes I did earlier. My mandate was clear. I was looking for a God-fearing woman. That was a huge deal breaker, and that's why I joined a Christian dating site. Her personality also mattered because she was going to be the first lady and had to interact with the church members.

The more I spoke to Sizakele, the more I liked her. But there was a problem. I was talking to another woman on the same app, and she was just as great. I had to make the difficult decision of choosing which lady would be the next Mrs. Chaplin. I will not lie and say it was an easy task.

I knew Sizakele was South African, and I had never been with anyone who was not American. I was a little nervous about the cultural difference, but we were compatible in so many other things. We both valued education and had obtained our master's degrees. We were both business-minded and wanted to achieve more in life. She loved to have children and build a family on Christian values, just like I did. I pictured a bright future with her and going on our first face-to-face date would be my deciding factor. Did we connect in person as we did over the phone? Did she look like she described herself in her profile and posted pictures? Not that her external appearances were going to change anything.

A couple of days before our first date, Sizakele asked to call me and wanted to discuss something really important with me. I remember thinking maybe she was no longer interested in me. As soon as we got on that video phone call, she asked me if I knew what Alopecia was? I said no! She asked me if I was okay if she told me more about it because she was living with the condition. I did not want to agree to something I had never heard about, so I asked her about what the condition was and how one gets it.

Siza took her time in breaking it down to me in layman's terms, and by the time she was done, I knew how Alopecia affected her. I could see how uncomfortable it made her feel to explain what Alopecia was. I was very empathetic towards her because I knew how it felt to have a condition in your body that you don't have control over. I was experiencing a similar situation but differently. So, I understood and felt her pain. I wanted to comfort her and take away the hurt she was feeling, but I understood that she had to do this for her healing. At that moment, I was supposed to offer her my undivided attention and give her the non-judgmental support she needed.

Siza was genuinely honest in her approach, and I loved that. It actually made me fall more in love with her. There is nothing sexier than an honest woman who knows her truth and story.

I could tell by the big sigh she took after explaining everything that a huge load was lifted off her shoulders. She was relieved that she did it and got it off her chest. Now the ball was in my court. My next response and reaction were going to either make or break this relationship. I knew this by how apprehensively she looked at me. I was not going to let her down. I needed to think before I said anything else because I didn't want to mess this up.

I then responded by saying, "It's okay. I understand, and I don't care what your hair looks like. I trust God will bring it back anyway. He is the restorer and healer, after all. I will continue to stand in the gap for you and pray with and for you for God's healing over your hair. In the meantime, know that I like you as you are, and I wouldn't change a thing about you. Hair is hair, and it does not define you.

You can show me what your head looks like whenever you feel comfortable, but please know that it will never change the way I feel about you.

Siza, you are a very beautiful and intelligent young lady, and I would be honored to take you out on our first official date. I wouldn't mind driving up to you in Connecticut, and we can go out for dinner at a restaurant of your choice this Sunday after church. Will that work for you?"

Sizakele

I was so humbled by how Leonard responded, and I knew this man was for keeps. He was so compassionate and considerate. I was ready to meet him.

Our first date was at the Olive Garden Italian Restaurant in Connecticut because that's where I was staying. He drove for two and a half hours to meet me in person. That made me feel special. The big day came, and I made an extra effort to look good. Nothing too hectic. I wore my modest knee-length black dress, showing a little cleavage, brown heel leather shoes, and my natural-looking wig. Leonard was smartly dressed in his black suit because he had come straight from church to see me. He was a gentleman, especially when he opened doors for me. I must say I was impressed.

He was already parked outside the restaurant when I arrived in an uber. I called him as I stepped out of the car, and we hugged each other so tight, as if we had met before. Meeting him felt right. I was comfortable with him. We had already spoken about almost everything via chatting on the dating app and on the phone, but now I felt at ease opening up to him even more. The only thing left on my side was to show him my scarred bald head. I felt ashamed and ugly, but he made me feel comfortable. I told him I would love to show him my head after dinner when he took me to my place.

Dinner was done, and Leonard paid. He surprised me because I heard you go 50-50 on dates in America. This guy kept on ticking the right boxes. He said and did all the right things. I was ready to show him my most shameful secret, my bald head with a few strands of hair left. As we drove closer to my apartment, my heart was beating faster and faster. I hadn't shown my head to anyone, including my family and friends. I needed to do this because I didn't want to get excited about this relationship only to scare him away after he saw what my head looked like. This was important, and his initial reaction would be a deal breaker.

As soon as he parked the car on the side of the road, he asked if he could kiss me.

"I really enjoyed myself with you", he said, "We should start planning our second date, but I would love to introduce you to my family. Thanksgiving is coming up soon, and that would be an excellent opportunity for you to meet them."

Boy, this man is moving fast. I have yet to show him my head. That's all I was thinking about while he kept on talking. I think it was the nerves that made me take off my wig to get his attention. I was looking down as I couldn't look him in the eyes. I didn't want to be disappointed by his initial reaction, although seeing it was important for me.

He slowly lifted my head and said, "I'm so sorry you are going through this. You will no longer go through it alone from now onwards. I know this is a painful time in your life, but I promise to be there for you every step of the way. You are beautiful, Sizakele, with or without hair. I still like you very much and know that God will heal you."

His response proved that he was the man I had been praying for. It sealed the deal. This man was for keeps; I was sure he was my forever after.

Needless to say, I met his family, and they liked me and approved. We got engaged on Christmas eve, a day before his 40th birthday. Three months later, we said our "I Do's" on my birthday, and seven years later, we are still blissfully in love. We also renewed our vows in South Africa on our 5th year anniversary. We did it the African traditional way this time and Leonard was thrilled and in awe of my culture. He wore his Zulu warrior (ibheshu) attire, and I wore my Zulu married women's cow skin attire and large red isicolo (African head gear for married women). You can check out our wedding on our YouTube channel 'Chilling with The Chaplins'.

Leonard

Meeting Sizakele, my African queen, my Awesomeness, has been life changing. We have had other challenges along our journey such as infertility and our businesses not taking off as speedily as we anticipated. However, we have not allowed that to put us down, but we have continued to love out loud and prove to many who were skeptical about online dating that it works just like any relationship if you put in the work. Unfortunately, some of my family members thought we wouldn't last and as a result they didn't even attend our wedding. This was very hurtful, but I knew I had married the love of my life and I had no regrets. I am happy to report that we now have full support of both our families and my family has embraced Siza with her hair loss because she has been the first one in our family to experience Alopecia. Siza has completely embraced her hair loss too and is now a global Alopecia ambassador that mentors, coaches, and counsels thousands of women around the world. She administrates a Facebook private group

'Global Alopecia Movement' and has self-published her debut book "Enough Already! Overcoming The Stigmas of Alopecia" available on Amazon and her website sizachaplin.com. She is also a dynamic inspirational public speaker who inspires many people with her vulnerable and empathetic approach. I am so proud of my wife and her achievements and look forward to many more blissful years together. We look forward to becoming parents too.

Lastly, I would like to advise that it is always best to be authentic and open as early as possible in your relationship. It helps to get the heavy stuff out of the way so you can concentrate on building a solid future.

Truth is…

Being open is important, and we really don't see it as taboo. In our own experiences, your reaction to any situation is going to set the standard for how someone responds to you. If you communicate your hair loss and the fact that you wear wigs or toppers in a way that's light and breezy, it shouldn't scare the other person away.

Whenever you decide to tell someone about your hair loss, anyone worth dating will understand that it's an important part of who you are that you're trusting them with. Whoever you are dating shouldn't feel the need to rush sharing it, either. This could be very controversial because some people might feel like you are hiding or lying, but at the end of the day, you should have to share this information only when you want to.

We understand that dating with hair loss may not feel as simple as it would without it, but it certainly shouldn't hold you back. The next time you catch yourself wondering what if your wig comes off during an intimate moment or whether the person, you're dating would even care about your hair loss, it's worth just asking them what they think. You never know how someone will react and who they really are unless you give them the opportunity to show you, and you might be pleasantly surprised.

We have all heard the famous saying that "love is blind" and Netflix has a reality show about this. The series follows single men and women searching for true love without seeing each other. "Love Is Blind" seeks to prove that real love results from intimate connections rather than superficial impressions.

We slightly disagree with this phrase and would rather say infatuation is blind. We believe that love is all-seeing and accepting. Love is seeing all the flaws and blemishes and accepting them. Love is accepting the bad habits and mannerisms and working around them. Love is recognizing all the fears and insecurities, and knowing your role is to comfort. Love is working through all the challenges and painful times. Infatuation is fragile and will shatter when life is not perfect. Love is strong and it strengthens because it is real.

> *Love is patient and kind; love does not envy or boast; it is not arrogant or rude. It does not insist on its own way; it is not irritable or resentful; it does not rejoice at wrongdoing but rejoices with the truth.*

1 Corinthians 13:4-8a (ESV)

I Live the Bald Life!

Meet the Chaplins

Leonard Chaplin, MBA is a Pastor, a certified Coach, Speaker, and Trainer of 'The John Maxwell Team'. He is very ambitious, with a strong appetite for education and learning. He completed four years of biblical school and is currently a Ph.D. candidate.

Leonard always dreamt of impacting the lives of young people, especially those from impoverished neighborhoods. He has a genuine passion to help others realize their significance, potential, and purpose. **Through his bold and deliberate messages, he desires to inspire people with untapped potential inside them to fulfill their God-given purpose.**

As a former party planner, he quickly realized that young people needed a safe haven and someone to believe in them and help direct or guide them towards their dreams and goals. Creating The Next Opportunity Window community, which gives people a safe place to have thought provoking conversations, sharing ideas and experiences where everyone can learn, grow, and connect with each other. He also introduced a Mentorship Boot Camp: Turn Your Ideas into a Sustainable/Scalable Business From Scratch program that helps individuals who are struggling to get started with their businesses.

One of his favorite quotes is *"No teaching, no revelation"* because he believes that practical, relevant teachings and programs can catalyze a person's transformation. In his spare time, he enjoys taking pictures with his wife and exploring different adventures.

Sizakele Mdluli-Chaplin, MBA is a dynamic international inspirational speaker, author, minister, content creator, and global Alopecia advocate and activist. She was born in the beautiful coastal city of Durban, South Africa – but now lives with her husband, a pastor, in New Jersey, United States.

Lady Siza as she is fondly known is called to serve women who have lost their self-worth and self-esteem. Her public speaking journey started after she was diagnosed with Alopecia. This auto-immune condition mistakenly attacks the hair follicles, thus causing the hair to fall out permanently in some cases like her own. She mentors and coach women worldwide by leading, inspiring, and teaching them to be the best they can be and live their lives with utmost boldness and honesty.

Siza has degrees in Environmental Health, Public Management, and Business. She self-published her first book 'Enough Already! Overcoming the stigmas of Alopecia'. She has also co-authored two Amazon bestseller books titled 'Phenomenal Women – Sisters Inspire Sisters' and 'Lemonade Chronicles.'

Siza loves to travel and is very adventurous.

Connect with Leonard:

Instagram: https://www.instagram.com/getinspired/

Community Website: https://nextopportunitywindow.com/

Website: www.chaplinlegacygroup.com

Email: getinspirebylj@gmail.com

Connect with Siza:

Instagram: https://www.instagram.com/ladysiza1/

Facebook: https://www.facebook.com/sizakele.mdluli.10

Website: www.sizachaplin.com

Email: sizachaplin@gmail.com

Photographer Credit: Rhonda Naicole
Instagram: @photographybyrhondanaicole

Beauford & Madinah Brown IV

We dedicate our chapter to our family, friends, co-workers, and everyone who supported us listened to and believed in us during this journey. We also dedicate this to each other. Over the years, we have supported and encouraged each other in our passions. We have created a beautiful relationship and loving family. ~ Mr. & Mrs. Brown

THE SECRETS TO MARRIAGE WITH ALOPECIA

"You were given this life because you are strong enough to live it!" ~ Unknown Author

Madinah's View

Growing up in a traditional Suni Muslim family, I began to wrap and wear a scarf/hijab at seven. It was a significant milestone for me. Hair was a big deal in a Muslim community, but not in the conventional sense! Because Islam sees covering of a woman's body as a form of modesty, only her immediate family or spouse could see her hair. By my teens, I couldn't remember life without the scarf on my head, and I didn't leave the house without it. I also never experienced going to a salon and getting my hair done. When I married my first husband at 18 years old, it was the first time in my life that I showed my hair to a male outside of my family.

After eight years of marriage and three children, I realized Islam was not my chosen path, but a path chosen for me, and I no longer wanted to follow this way of living. I decided to enroll in college and began to explore the idea of going out without my scarf. The day I finally dared to be in the world without covering my head, I felt as if I had gone outside without clothes! This feeling was magnified when I went to my first class that week without my scarf; it felt like all eyes were on me. Like everyone knew, I was supposed to be wearing a scarf and had chosen not to and had gone against my parents and my religion! This was not the case, but the stress of this was tremendous.

At the same time, my relationship with my husband became more abusive to the point where I finally acknowledged I needed to leave for my and my children's sake! After our separation, my stress level went even higher, and I began to have severe pain and uncontrollable itching on my scalp, which even kept me up at night. Every time I had to remove the weave; my scalp was so tender that it was painful to touch. I attributed this to wearing braids/weaves and pushed forward. Then at one of my hair appointments, my stylist told me she found a spot at the back of my head. She asked me if I had noticed any shedding or hair loss, and I said *yes*, but I thought it was the usual amount after removing the braids. As the months went by, the spot got larger, and one spot became two, three, and four. I began to panic with fear and shame!

To make matters worse, I was in the middle of a divorce, had left my religion and the support of my family, and was now a single mom in college with three children on her own. I began to believe that this, in some way, was a punishment from God. That I had sinned, and because of it, I would lose my hair. I did everything possible to hide the hair loss from everyone, including my family and especially my new boyfriend, Beauford. I prayed at every hair appointment that my stylist would tell me my hair had started to grow back or at least had stopped falling out, but of course, that did not happen. Finally, at one appointment, she told me that the patches had become so much that she could barely cover them and that she thought I should see a dermatologist so I could figure out what was happening. It was devastating, but I eventually found the courage to see a doctor. Deep down, I knew something was wrong. When I got the diagnosis after my biopsy, I was shocked. I had never heard of Alopecia, and learning it was permanent was heartbreaking.

By this time, Beauford and I had been dating for about two years, and my worse fear was that he would somehow find out and leave me. I did everything I could to hide my hair loss from him. I made sure he never saw me without my braids or extensions/weaves. And when I had to get my hair redone, I would lock myself in a bathroom to take out my hair and wear a scarf or bandana to the salon. I also never let him touch my hair or head, even when we were intimate. I thought that even if he felt the spots in the dark, he would know. It was truly exhausting trying to hide so much from someone so close.

Beauford's View

When Madinah and I met, her hair was always in long braids. After several months of dating, I found a picture of Madinah and noticed her hair was thinning. It was easily noticeable along the sides of her head. I was shocked, not because the thinning looked terrible, but because I couldn't believe I had no clue she was dealing with hair loss. I also didn't know if the hair loss was permanent or what was causing it. I don't believe she had even mentioned the hair loss up to that point. Nothing was anchoring me to stay. I owed Madinah no compassion or empathy and we didn't share children at this point. All I knew was I felt a deeply connected to Madinah. From the moment I met her, I felt there was something special about her. I loved so many things about her. It was an easy decision for me to stay in my relationship and not mention that I knew about her hair loss. So, I put the picture back and continued to love her.

Madinah's View

Years into our relationship, I decided to share my hair loss with my husband. We had one child together and another on the way, not including my three children from my previous marriage. Throughout the years, I had shared bits and pieces, letting him know I had thinning or a spot here or there, but I never told him my diagnosis, and I NEVER let him see me without a weave or extensions. But after eight years together and our second baby on the way, I told him that my dermatologist wanted me to stop wearing the weaves to let the inflammation go down on my scalp. Also, I could barely cover the spots because I had lost so much hair. I remember telling him I had Alopecia and explaining that my hair loss was permanent. I began to cry, and he just held me and said, *"It is ok"!*

My fear at this point wasn't that he would reject me or scream with freight; it was more the fear of vulnerability. This person would now truly know me and all of my imperfections. The freighting idea was that once he sees me this way, he can never unsee it, and what if I was no longer the beautiful image of the woman he married! These thoughts and more went through my head a million times before, and that's why I didn't share them with him for so long. But the reality was my fear came from the fact that I didn't see beauty in myself without my hair, so I didn't think anyone else could, especially not a man. When I finally showed him my hair for the first time, I felt raw and naked. He was extremely gentle with his words, and I could tell he didn't want to hurt me. I wore a wig for several months and slowly began to feel more comfortable about him seeing me in this form. Then one day, I decided I wanted to shave what little hair was left. So, at about eight months pregnant, I told my husband. And he shaved my head in our bathroom with our three girls. These were the most freeing and liberating moments I can remember, and I truly felt joy! But when I looked up, I saw my girls crying. I comforted them and told them I was not sad. They said that I was so brave, and they were so proud of me. This moment marked the beginning of my journey to truly love and accept myself and display it in a way that my daughters can understand what that looks like!

Even when I got to the point where I knew I wanted to go out without a wig or accessory, I still was terrified of what other people would think of me. No matter how much my husband and children told me I was beautiful, I knew I didn't feel it in myself, and I couldn't believe that total strangers would feel the same as my family. Part of this was how people commented on my hair when I wore wigs and extensions. However, one experience was that last drop that pushed me out of hiding. One day, I met with a vendor who the last time he saw me I had braids. Since then, I had transitioned to a short pixie wig. He waited for the end of the day while we were saying our goodbyes to approach me in my office and began complimenting me on my hair. At first, I thought nothing of it, and then he continued and began to explain that he thought I looked so professional with my new hairstyle and that the braids had made me look like the "girl next door," but now I was "beautiful"! As he continued, all I could think was, *"if he only knew that this was a wig and I was truly bald with Alopecia, what would he think of me then?"* All at once, I became angry, sad, and ashamed. I wanted to scream at him about his ignorance, assumptions, and stereotypes, but I was gripped with fear about my secret being "found out." So, when he left, I broke down in tears of shame. After this experience, I realized I didn't want to hide my true self anymore. I wanted the world to see me as I was and judge me from there. So, I planned to remove my wig once and for all.

I decided to first tell my boss and coworkers; this was more comfortable for me because I work in HR. They were all supportive and wanted to help in any way they could. Then I choose a date to announce it to my company. I don't believe this was necessary, but I thought it would save me the persistent questions if I just came into work one day bald. I then began to go out on the weekends around town without my wig to build my confidence in public before I shared it with my company. The date I chose to share was at a company event, so I could ensure that most employees would be there, and they all could see and ask questions at once. I wish I could say that it was a great experience with no regrets, but it was not perfect, that is for sure.

I had a few comments that really stung, but for the most part, it went pretty smoothly. Once it was over, I felt like a huge weight was lifted, but that is when the real work began for me. Every day when I came home from work, I felt raw. I felt as if I had shared myself with the world, and even though I knew there would be comments, stares, whispers, and more random strangers giving me medical advice, I somehow felt unprepared each day. I wanted to hide and be invisible and small, but the more I felt that way, it seemed, the more it happened. After about a week or two of going without my hair, I decided to address the ugly truth in me. I was not ok with how I looked. I felt unattractive and ugly. And I couldn't see how anyone wouldn't see otherwise. Friends suggested that I start to journal my feelings and emotions each day. Still, by the end of my days, I was so exhausted mentally and emotionally that I would immediately come home and go straight to the bathroom to cry. And I would make sure never to look at myself in the mirror. I knew I couldn't go on this way and needed to address my self-image, but I didn't know how to start. Then one day after work, as I stood in the mirror, I began to stare at myself and say words of affirmation, *"you are beautiful," "you are loved,"* etc. This experience led me to take pictures of myself each day I came home. I began to start a photo journal of my experience. I realized it was much easier to look at myself in a photo than in the mirror, and I could begin seeing the beauty!

Beauford's View

At first, knowing the right decision in many situations was difficult. I defaulted to being as supportive as possible, but I always tried to be honest with Madinah without hurting her feelings. Honestly, I wouldn't say I liked many of the wigs my wife wore for various reasons. I preferred Madinah to wear braids. However, I knew about the damage that braids caused to her scalp. Also, on a couple of occasions, people commented on how professional she looked with her wig. So, I kept my preferences to myself.

Madinah and I discussed her going without wigs for a few months before she finally got the confidence to allow me to cut her hair. I experienced mixed emotions. On the one hand, I was so happy for her as she was finally confident enough to face her fear. On the other hand, I was secretly terrified; I considered myself a protector of my family and did not want to see my wife hurt. So, I had to constantly remind myself to allow Madinah to speak for herself. I would stand by, trying not to have an angry face while people mentioned Madinah's choice to display her bald head. To my surprise, most people were kind. They were genuinely curious, so it opened opportunities for discussion and education about Alopecia. I'm so happy I was wrong about what role I would play in Madinah's everyday interactions with the world. Have there been inappropriate comments? Of course, but for the most part, people have been kind.

Madinah's View

When I look back on my journey with Alopecia, I wonder about the things I would have done differently or what I wish someone had told me early on. I wish I had trusted the love of my husband and children from the beginning and saved myself from years of hiding in shame! And I wish I had sought professional help early to deal with my self-image and my struggle with my hair and religious beliefs. I feel that all of these things would have been so beneficial in my growth and journey. Also, it would have been helpful to know the stories of other people who faced Alopecia. Living in fear and pain alone is too much for one person to carry. Thus, hearing about the pain, fears, and triumphs of others would bring the feeling that there are people who are going through a similar experience.

Beauford's View

My first perception of Madinah from our first conversation was that she's sexy, confident, and brave. I built her into my superhero future wife. Finding out that she was hiding hair loss from me temporarily changed my perspective of her. I had to acknowledge that she feared telling me. She felt vulnerable, and I could only assume she hid it because she thought I might leave her.

Over the years, I have watched my wife grow into an amazing woman. I'm so glad I decided to stay when I found that picture. As we grew in our relationship, I felt like we grew closer with every bit of admission from my wife. She leaned on me when she felt vulnerable, or someone made an inappropriate comment. What makes me happy is that my wife doesn't hide who she is from anyone.

Madinah's View

It has been five years since I first stopped wearing my wig, and a lot has changed in my relationship with myself. The first year was the hardest as I learned to become comfortable with my new look and with the reality of living with Alopecia. I wake up each morning and am no longer afraid to look in the mirror and see myself. I feel like I have my life back and no longer have this secret or fear when I go out. Yes, I have bad days like any person, but those days are few and far between. Most days, I genuinely forget that I am bald when I am out in public until I see a look from someone who stops me and asks about my head.

My relationship with my husband has also grown stronger because of my decisions. When I started going out without my wig he would often try to be close to me in case someone said or did something hurtful. And we would have many discussions about how people's reactions in public made me feel. But as I became more comfortable, I could feel him relax as well.

Not all of the attention was negative, though; more and more, I would get men and women approaching me to tell me how beautiful I was, how brave and strong, and how they could never do what I was doing. Some of these people were living with Alopecia secretly, and some had family and friends with it. These comments helped build my confidence, but at first, even this was too much for me. And then I started to become used to it, but I would respond and say that I wasn't brave, or I didn't feel beautiful but thank you. And because of this, I had strangers tell me to stop and truly look at myself and how what I was doing was helping others. Of course, this attitude began to stick with me, and I began to see what they were seeing. Now when people - young or old, bald or with hair - stop me to compliment my beauty and baldness, I smile and say thank you, and if they are curious, I am more than happy to explain to them that I have Alopecia and what that is.

I watched my husband go from being concerned for me and wanting to protect me whenever I left the house to being the confident man I married. I recently asked him whether it bothers him that we are often stopped by men and women (sometimes even in the middle of dinner) to talk about my hair. He said, *"No, it has never bothered me; the only time it bothered me was when I knew it bothered you, and I will always welcome compliments that help boost your confidence!"* You see, knowing where we are today in our marriage and relationship, I look back and think, why was I ever afraid to share this with the most important person in my life? If I could share anything with couples going through this journey, I would say don't be afraid to share and be open and vulnerable. And for the supporting spouse, let your partner lead the journey and go as fast or slow as they are comfortable. It is hard to pinpoint all the little things that may or may not change in your relationship, but ultimately, this is a journey that both of you will go through together!

Beauford's View

Madinah and I have had many ups and downs in our relationship, but I am proud to say that I rarely think about her Alopecia. I have supported her in her advocacy and hope to continue to do so. Every project we participate in, I believe, strengthens our bond. We each pour our hearts into sharing a part of our life. We are no different than any other husband and wife. I desire my wife just as much today as I did when we first met. I hope it shows through my contributions to Madinah's attempts to share her story and uplift others.

Here are some valuable lessons we have learned on this journey that will help you on yours…

1. **It's ok to be vulnerable**! I feel as black women and women in general, we think that we always need to be strong, and any type of vulnerability is a weakness! But this is not the case; sometimes the strongest person is the person who can allow themselves to be vulnerable and allow others to support and love them!

2. **Trust your circle**. If you have family and friends that love and care about you, trust them enough to share your story and your journey. I feel that in hiding my Alopecia from my family and friends for so long, not only did I have to suffer in silence and hide, but I also robbed them of the opportunity to grieve with me.

3. **Find a community**. After I shared my diagnosis with my family and friends, I swore that I didn't need a "support group" even when everyone around me tried to encourage me to join one. I felt like I would somehow not be accepted. That maybe I didn't lose enough hair, or I had the wrong type of Alopecia or that my journey wasn't a "struggle/hardship". So, I spent months trying

to convince myself that I had made it this far and I could do it alone. But when I eventually did meet my Alopecia support group, I had a feeling of likeness and acceptance that I could not get from my friends and family.

4. **Ask & Share.** This advice might sound like an easy one, but I had to learn to ask my husband difficult questions, like "do you still find me attractive" "how do you prefer to see me" "how do you feel when people stare" "are you ever ashamed of my hair loss"? And because I learned to do this, we were able to truly communicate and be open and honest. Although this is my hair loss journey, he is on this journey with me as my husband, and the last thing I want is to not know how he truly feels about me. This communication is a very scary thing because you need to be completely vulnerable, but I believe this is the number one thing that strengthened our marriage and relationship!

"The most important thing is to find a way to accept and love yourself in your true form, and the rest in life will follow" – Madinah Brown

I Live the Bald Life!

Meet the Browns

Beauford Ulysses Brown IV is a US Army reserve Retiree and currently holds a position with the Squaxin Island Tribe as an IT Regulatory. He is a father of six and spends most of his time outside work as the family chauffeur.

He strives to provide his wife and children with an environment that supports mental, emotional, and physical growth.

As such, Beauford is launching a family business, Brown Family Hauling and Junk Removal. This business will provide services to friends, family, and the surrounding community. It also allows him to lead his family in a new direction toward entrepreneurship.

In his free time, Beauford enjoys photography, hiking, and gardening.

Madinah Brown is a wife and mom of six exceptional children. As the Benefit and Training Manager of Harbor Wholesale, she oversees the healthcare administration and vendor relationships. She provides expertise and insight into employee benefits programs for the organization. She also plans various projects to promote health and wellness for employees.

She is an avid volunteer for projects in her community, such as the Crazy Faith Homeless Project, Habitat for Humanity, and the Alopecia Support Group in Seattle, Washington. She has also been featured in the Awarding Documentary – Harmony: Alopecia Series.

Madinah is a contributing author in "bald life" magazine and is working on her autobiography. In her spare time, she loves spending time outdoors and bike riding. She spends summers hiking and camping with her family in the Pacific Northwest.

Connect with Beauford:

Facebook: https://www.facebook.com/beauford.brown?mibextid=ZbWKwL

Email: Beauford.brown@yahoo.com

Instagram: https://www.instagram.com/beauford_nutty_buddy_brown/

Connect with Madinah:

LinkedIn: http://www.linkedin.com/in/madinah-brown-45b0133a

Email: mmujib32@gmail.com

Photographer Credit: Chazton Anderson

Website: 1029photography.com

Email: 1029photographyllc@gmail.com

HENRY & DOMINIQUE COOPER

I dedicate this chapter to my wife, Dominique Wimbush Cooper. My helpmate, my friend and my good thing. You have been a constant source of inspiration and encouragement to me. Your love is endless and pure. Thank you for loving me and I hope you've enjoyed this journey together as much as I have. ~ Mr. Cooper

    I dedicate my chapter to Stephanie Sloan for being the best motivator and encourager. For allowing me to cry on her shoulder but never letting me dwell in my sorrow. For consistently reminding me that if I continue to just be me, I'll always be enough, with or without hair. ~ Mrs. Cooper

FROM LYME TO LIMEADE

"Never be limited by other people's limited imaginations."

– **Dr. Mae Jamison**

Her Story

Allow me to introduce myself. I'm Dominique Cooper from Richmond, VA. I'm a stay-at-home mom to a service dog named Peppy. She's off the charts cute and smart but nowhere close to our nephew and two sweet granddaughters. They are my heartbeats and call me "Honey"… told you they're sweet!

I celebrated 25 years of marriage this past September to an amazingly loving man of God (Lee). And guess what... he's my best friend, business partner, and caretaker! My husband and I are co-founders of a small Gluten-Free skincare business called Honey's Natu-Raw, LLC.

Here's my story...

One day in January 1992, I woke up on my sofa feeling very heavy and weird. As I slowly rolled over, I saw two huge televisions, but I knew only one was really there. The images were far apart, and I couldn't tell which was the correct one. As I started getting up, I noticed that I was extremely dizzy and had an unimaginable headache. Being home alone, I asked my neighbor to take me to Patient First. The physician told me I had a virus and scheduled an appointment with a neurologist in a few days. By the time of my appointment, my right eye was huge, protruding, and stuck in the most awkward position. After days of testing and another visit to the neurologist, I was diagnosed with Optical Neuritis / Cranial Pseudo Tumor. On that day, my neurologist took me out of work for the next seven months. I guess he knew that it would take that long to get a solution. So, I started going from hospitals to doctor's appointments and doing pervasive testing. They did all kinds of biopsies, spinal taps, MRIs, etc. I felt like a guinea pig. Then one day, out of nowhere, my vision started coming back after seven months of having double vision and bad headaches. Little by little, my body started lining up. And just as my neurologist predicted, I returned back to work in July. I thought everything was better until I realized that my hair had started to thin drastically during the past seven months.

A few weeks later, I was going to see one of my favorite groups in concert. I'd gotten my hair done in the infamous "French Roll," but while dressing, I couldn't stop scratching my scalp. The itching was like nothing that I'd experienced before. It was one hundred times worse than the annoying itching that I'd been having over the past several weeks. I began to scratch so uncontrollably that my hair was coming out into my hands. Panic gripped me. Somehow, I still managed to make my hair look presentable for the concert. However, I sat and cried in misery and silence the entire time. The next day, I scheduled an appointment with a dermatologist, who told me I was putting too much pressure on my hair follicles, recommended using the cream prescribed, and assured me that everything would be OK. I took the doctor's advice, and the itching improved, but despite all my efforts, the thinning worsened. I saw many other dermatologists desperately seeking help and hoping to get my hair back. Finally, I found someone that could help me. However, by that time, the hair loss was so significant that the best that the dermatologist could tell me was to leave it alone and not put any pressure on my scalp. Unfortunately, there was nothing more that she could do. At that very moment, all hope was lost. It was final. The hair that I'd lost wasn't going to come back. I sat in my car and cried for about fifteen minutes and then I did what I do best.... I suppressed it.

The only person that knew what I was going through was one of my besties. I knew I could be vulnerable with her, and she wouldn't make me feel any worse with pity. She would help me find a solution while encouraging me to stay strong.

Well, I'd heard about a woman who specialized in creating healthy styles to cover hair loss in women. So, I met with her for a consultation, and she explained the procedure. She also advised me that her technique caused little to no tugging on the scalp. The only problem was that it would be a lot of hair, which just gave me all kinds of anxiety because I knew that it would be impossible for anyone not to notice the drastic change. I shared through tears how sad I was about coming to work with all this hair on my head with my girlfriend. She said, "It doesn't matter how much hair she has to add as long as it looks good, and when you come to work, just be Doma (what my besties call me), and I promise you'll be just fine." Her words were life-changing for me, and I'll never forget them. I did just as she said. I embraced her words and just continued to be me! Sharing my story of how I dealt with my Alopecia is the key factor that got me through it. I was also a single parent at the time and didn't want my son to see me sad, so I suppressed it deep down inside me. I really believe that's how I survived it. I'm sure that people were talking, but no one ever questioned me. I truly believe that was God's way of shielding me and allowing me to cope with that horrendous nightmare.

At that time, I still had a lot of hair, but it was extremely thin at the crown. One day after a shower while I was getting ready for work, the itching started again. I didn't think it could ever be worse than it had been in the past, but it was. I spent the entire morning weeping as I scratched out over 80% of my hair that was left. I called my friend at work, and when she answered, I hysterically cried and screamed, "All of my hair is gone, and I feel so ugly." She calmly said, "Go ahead and cry it out, but we just have to continue to search for solutions, and Doma, you could never be ugly".

For many years after that, I confidently hid under very expensive weaves and hair replacement systems. I have to admit that I was very comfortable in them. I wore them as if the hair was growing from my scalp. However, whenever it was time to have it redone, I would go into a mini depression with anxiety for the entire time I was in my stylist's chair. I would be praying and asking God to please let it look nice and prevent others from seeing my secret. In fact, I couldn't tell anybody how my scalp looked for a million dollars. I also refused to look at it as I knew that it would only depress me. Immediately after it was done, I'd go right back to being happy Dominique.

I met my husband on a blind phone date in September 1996. We talked on the phone for eight weeks before seeing each other. When we met face to face, I was wearing a weave, but he NEVER asked me one question about my hair. We were married twelve months later.

In July of 2007, I started getting very sick with all these weird and debilitating symptoms. Then in January of 2008, I had my first of two mini-strokes. The next one was in November of same year. And after countless seizures and thirteen Chronic Illnesses/Autoimmune diagnoses in August of 2009, I was diagnosed with Chronic Lyme Disease. Lyme Disease is extremely difficult to detect, and if left untreated, it can attack every body part. By the time I was diagnosed correctly, Lyme Disease had already induced Type 1 Diabetes (multiple organs), Celiac Disease (intestines), Small Fiber Neuropathy (brain/neurological system), Fibromyalgia (muscle, ligaments, connective tissue, brain) and Tick-Borne Alopecia Areata (skin/hair loss).

My Lyme and Celiac treatment require me to rid my body and home of as many toxins as possible and to adhere to a 100% Gluten Free diet. So, I started deeply researching and learning how to make body and home care products after realizing that there were little to no acceptable shelf products for me to use.

As I mentioned before, I wore expensive hair replacement units and systems for many years. But I started having awful sensory issues and paresthesia (overwhelming feelings of things under my skin, such as pins and needles, tingling, and an intense continuous buzzing). I became very sensitive to certain fabrics, and the hair units were now bothering me. Also, the prices were rising, and the quality was falling. I kept sharing with my husband how upset and dissatisfied I was. And he kept telling me to shave it off. He assured me that it wouldn't matter to him because he would love me the same with or without hair. And in May of 2018, with my husband by my side, I bravely decided to shave my head. With my newfound freedom, I felt so beautiful and confident! Unfortunately, the very next morning, I had unsightly and painful razor bumps. I knew I had sensitive skin, but this was a painful crime scene. Then I realized that the bumps and irritation would occur each time I shaved, no matter how careful I was. Also, my scalp had some blemishes and discoloration. Fortunately, I'd already learned how to formulate body care products that were safe for my skin in 2016 when we established Honey's Natu-Raw. So, I returned to the lab to start the journey of formulating products to care for my shaved head. The formula needed to work for the face as well. As baldies, we treat the scalp and face as one.

As with all our products, my greatest challenge was to formulate a plant-based system that would reduce or, at best, eliminate the problems I was experiencing. After fourteen months of trial and error, FREE DOME®, a scalp and face care system for Brave, Bald, Beauties, and Bros, was born. Our FREE DOME® System is free of Synthetic ingredients, including fragrances, sulfates, parabens, phthalates, and formaldehyde-forming preservatives. All of our ingredients are 100% Gluten-Free, and the products are made in a Gluten Free environment, making them perfect for Celiac sufferers.

It is handmade with joy by a chemically sensitive Baldie for other Alopecians and Baldies.

Our FREE DOME®. Consists of a two-piece system:

1. Invigorating Scalp and Face Cleanser

2. Daily Restorative Scalp and Face Oil

Our natural and organic ingredients are carefully chosen to meet the needs of a shaved scalp. Our Daily Restorative Scalp and Face Oil can also be used on other shaved areas such as armpits and bikini lines. We've considered nicks, bumps, scrapes, and other irritations from shaving. This Scalp and Face Care System was tailored-made for a FREE DOME.®.

Lee and I are constantly amazed at what God has given us because neither of us takes any credit for this marvelous creation. We're just vessels used to help encourage others when they're ready to walk in their FREE DOME®. Each of our products has a scripture (John 8:32) on the front of the bottle along with encouraging subliminal messages around the ribbon, such as Get Free, Own It, Be Free, Walk in It, and Live Free.

We love saying that we were blessed to turn Lyme Disease into Limeade. FREE DOME®.

Free Indeed

His Story

What can you do when you're born with a receding hairline that will only get worse? I didn't know I had one or was any different from other guys until I was told about it. I had to endure joke after joke after joke. Starting in elementary school with kids saying to me, "You got a big forehead!!", the jokes continued in middle school, then in high school, and in the military. Later I faced numerous jokes from fellow employees on jobs I've had. These people, boys, girls, men and women comedians, jokers, bullies, or so-called friends, have bullied or teased me about my hairline all my life.

The older I got, the more my hairline receded, and I was more aware of it. I wore caps and hats whenever I could to cover it up, especially around those bullies and jokesters. I was really embarrassed about it. Even when no one would say anything, I still felt like they noticed it and were thinking about it. I mean, it was right there in their face. I was self-conscious.

There was a time when I do believe my hair stopped receding. From my time in the Marine Corps 1982-1988 (in my early twenties) until my early thirties 1992-1995, the joking and bullying had stopped, or the people around me, and I didn't notice it. Also, during this time, I was building a relationship with the Most-High God and probably just wasn't focused on my hair or others' behaviors toward me. God had my focus, all of it!!

I met my best friend, lover, and wife, Dominique, in 1996. We hit it off from the top. We talked on the phone for eight weeks without laying eyes on one another, and I just knew that this lady and I would be something special. When I finally met her (after she stole my heart on the phone), I was numb to the fact that my receding hairline existed. We were so deep in love that it really wouldn't have mattered. She would accept me as I was, and I would accept her the same. The foundation for love and support was set.

In September of 1997, on the 6th day, we were happily married. I was comfortable around her, but the old ashamed me (the receding hairline) was back around others. I wore my caps and hats everywhere. To hide my head and its receding hairline, which was way back.

Then one day, I was just finished holding on to my receding hairline and the points that started nearly in the middle of my head. Gentleman, you know how you get that round-up with the nice points at the temples around the ears and neck. Well, my points were literally going from the middle of the top of my head to my temples. This time I felt the clippers up there, and I told my barber, "Hold on, let me see that mirror." He handed me the mirror, and I looked at the top and sides of my head. I was disgusted and ashamed of what I saw. I told him I needed to make a call. I called Dominique, and I told her that I was going to cut it off and she said, "Cut it off, Handsome Chocolate" (she calls me that often). I went back to the chair and said, "Man, cut this mess off my head. I'm not walking around anymore with my points back to the middle of my head. That's crazy". He asked me if I was sure, and I responded, "for sure."

When he finished, I was like, wow, why did I wait so long to do this, man? It doesn't look bad at all. He said, "I'll probably lose you as a customer, though." I replied, "No way, you still have dibs on my facial hair". We laughed.

Although I was given the green light to cut it, I wasn't sure what my Honey was going to think once she saw it. In my eyes, altering my appearance like that was a big deal. But as usual, she showed nothing but support, words of inspiration, and encouragement. She is the BOMB, and I love her for that. I am more comfortable with my bald head than I was with my hair. You see, with the hair, you could see the receding but that's not visible anymore.

I'll never forget the day my wife shaved her head. We were at a Salon, vending our skincare products, and she walked up to me and said, "I'm going to do it". I asked, "Do what"? "Shave it all off" she said, and she did it. She looked and still looks beautiful in her Free Dome. I just love it. The only problem was now she would have to learn to shave and treat her scalp. After a few attempts using my shaving cream and type of razors, she decided that she would create something natural and healing for her scalp. She also needed it to be gluten-free as she has Celiac Disease. She finalized her formula approximately a year later, and FREE DOME® (our scalp and face care system) was born. I am a co-founder of FREE DOME®, overseeing the logistics (product labeling, shipping, receiving, etc.). This business was born from a need. We've just been sharing the goodness with others that struggle to find products that are gluten-free and non-toxic.

FREE DOME® is a blessing; we know it is inspired and sent by GOD. We had no intentions of having a skincare business at all. Yet here we are sharing and providing our Scalp and Face care systems while encouraging others to be free.

We both agree that had we known each other all those years ago, suffering from Alopecia would not have been as great. Although difficult, the bald life journey is much easier because we unconditionally love one another. Excepting each other for who we are and not how we look has deepened our respect for each other. We hope that our stories will encourage other couples that may be facing Alopecia to give unwavering support.

If you are bald and experiencing scalp irritation, try these tips:

- Treat your scalp before shaving by covering your face and head with a warm towel before and after shaving
- Use a pre-shave oil
- Always use shaving cream, gel or butter
- Moisturize immediately after shaving

Use products free of fragrance, sodium lauryl sulfate, alcohol, glycols, and parabens

We Live the Bald Life!

Meet The Coopers

Henry L. Cooper is a God-loving and God-fearing man who loves traveling and the ocean. He enjoys playing chess and any brain-teasing games. He served in the United States Marine Corps as a Jet Mechanic and Plane Captain. While serving in the military, Henry had a chance to travel to many different places. He has lived in Tennessee, South Carolina, California, and Hawaii. He has traveled to Tokyo, Hiroshima, Iwakuni, Okinawa, Japan, Osan, Pusan Korea, and Philippine Islands.

Henry has an associate degree in Computer Programming from ECPI University, worked as a computer programmer, and is currently in his 21st year at a Fortune 500 company. He is also a contributing author to Living the Bald Life Anthology.

He met his beautiful wife, Dominique, on a blind date. They talked on the telephone for eight weeks before seeing one another, which helped to build a friendship that would become one of the foundational blocks, along with their commitments to the Lord and their relationship.

They were married within eleven months of meeting and celebrated their 25th wedding anniversary on September 6, 2022. They have a son DaVon and two gorgeous granddaughters, Nia and Siah, who they love spending time with, laughing, encouraging, and inspiring to be their best versions.

They love to share and pour into others, especially married couples. They created the "Covenant Couples Ministry," which allows couples to grow by focusing on the things they might be taking for granted. It's a fun and loving experience with complete confidentiality. They are looking forward to walking in the purpose they were created for, Loving Love, keeping couples happy in their marriages, and showing them how to fight for it somewhat. They date every Friday night and have been doing so consistently for the past 25 years.

2014 they created "Order My Steps," a business that helps couples and loved ones get their vital life documents together for easy access when they are or will be needed. (Insurances, deeds, wills, etc.)

They are co-owners of Free Dome, formerly Honey's Natu-Raw, a gluten-free skincare brand created in 2016. It was made with the Alopecian, Celiac, Diabetic, Eczema, Fibromyalgia, and Lyme Disease communities in mind. They are gluten-free due to celiac disease and try to live non-toxic lives. They are looking forward to expanding in 2023 by adding a Nourishing Shaving Soap Bar to their Scalp and Face Care Line.

The experience of sharing his story through Living the Bald Life Anthology has been a blessing, and he hopes that his story helps someone heal. He believes that his purpose on this earth has nothing to do with him but everything to do with what his creator can do through him.

Dominique "Honey" Cooper co-founded Honey's Natu-Raw, LLC- a Gluten-Free skincare brand. Together with her husband and partner Lee, they formulate non-toxic, organic, natural, and Gluten Free face and body care products.

In 2018 they launched "FREE DOME"®, a two-piece scalp and face care system explicitly formulated for Alopecians and Baldies. They're both very active in the Alopecia community and have become advocates. Dominique dedicates much of her time encouraging hair loss sufferers like herself to embrace their FREE DOME®. She's created an Instagram and Facebook page called OurFreeDome, where she features women, children, and men that have lost their hair and are now owning and walking in their FREE DOME®. The Coopers have a YouTube channel called OurFreeDome, where they share tips and pointers on living Gluten-Free and toxin-free lives.

Having been married for 25 years, the Coopers are passionate about helping other married couples achieve a happy and successful union. In 2016 they started The Covenant Couples Ministry. Each quarter they host an event for married couples to come together in a safe space to share their strengths and weaknesses. They stand on the biblical principles that "Iron Sharpens Iron" (Pr 27:7) and "What God has put together, let no man put asunder" (Matt 19:6).

In January 2014, the Coopers launched "Order My Steps," where they help others to organize all of their essential documents from banking to wills. It's a four-hour event; everyone leaves with a binder that conveniently houses their life documents in one place.

Although she loves helping others, Dominique finds the most joy in serving God, traveling, Friday date nights, and spending time with her granddaughters. They named her Honey!

Connect with Henry

Website: www.honeysnaturaw.com

Instagram: https://www.instagram.com/bald_coo_free/

Connect with Dominique

Facebook: https://www.facebook.com/dominique.cooper.313

Instagram: https://www.instagram.com/iamdominiquecooper/

YouTube: https://youtube.com/@ourfreedome.9131

Website: www.honeysnaturaw.com

The Visionary
Jamie Elmore

This chapter is dedicated to my amazing family who has supported me every step of the way. To my daughter who is the epitome of resilience and strength. To my sister who speaks life into me and believes in every idea that I share with her. To my mother my biggest cheerleader.

THE MIRROR

"Our Story is Not Our Story; Our Story is for someone else" ~ Jamie Elmore

I am a woman, daughter, sister, mother, and friend. I am a fighter, innovator, speaker, author, and visionary. I am a child of God! I have a story that I am responsible for sharing so I can help someone else. I invite you to take a ride with me, understanding that you have a story as well. Our story is different, but it needs to be told. I encourage you to be open-minded and think about your experiences in life and how my story can propel you into making a positive impact on the lives of others.

My Love for hair

When I was a young girl, my Christmas list always included a doll. I loved to play in my doll's hair. When I was in the fourth grade, I braided my own hair. By the time I was in the seventh grade, I knew I wanted to be a hairstylist and open a hair salon. As I grew older, I would style my friends and family's hair. On Sundays after church, I would have the deaconess and choir members lined up in an assembly line one after another to style their hair from updo's to French rolls and French braids; you name it, I did it. I felt like I was born to do hair!

My Dream came true

I graduated from Garfield High school in 1987, and in 1991, at the age of 21, I finally received my cosmetology license and my dream of becoming a hairstylist had come true.

1993

In August 1993, I received the news that I was pregnant. I was disappointed in myself because I was raised in the church, and it was custom that you be married before you have children. I was not married, and I felt like I committed the ultimate sin. Having sex out of wedlock! I knew I would bust hell wide open! I was afraid of what my parents and my church community would say and think of me. However, when I shared the news with my parents, they were supportive. My Dad asked were me and boyfriend (at the time) getting married? We had the conversation and I'm glad we never did. I was attending NCCC, New Covenant Christian Center in Seattle, WA, during that time. I decided to talk to my pastors, and they also spoke words of love and support.

It was Wednesday night bible study, November 24, 1993, Thanksgiving eve. I was sitting in the chair, and Pastor Tony finished up his sermon and asked me to come up to the front of the church so he and Pastor Renee could pray for me and my pregnancy. Now that was the first time my church family heard of me being pregnant. I froze and felt like I was about to swallow my tongue literally. They prayed heaven down!

911

On Christmas eve of the same year, my parents and I were coming home from our family gathering. I felt something wet running down my leg. So, when we entered the house, I went to the restroom. I screamed because I was bleeding. My mother busted the door open, saw the blood, and immediately called 911. My parents drove me to the hospital, where I was seen by a few doctors and told that I would be put on bed rest until I could give birth. Janiece was scheduled to be born in April 1994.

As I began to get settled into my new "home" (the hospital) for the next couple of months, my situation took another turn for the worse. I started to have contractions. The doctors did not want me to give birth; it was too early. They tried everything but to no avail. My family and friends were standing around my bedside, praying, and my friend Toya began to sing a song titled "Bless your name, Lord". The peace of God filled my hospital room, and the nurses said they had never experienced anything like that before. Three hours into my contractions, my daughter's heart rate was showing signs of stress. I was told that I would have to have an emergency c-section. My daughter was born on December 30, 1993, at 25 weeks, weighing 1lb 8.8ozs. She was a pound of flour, and you could put her entire body in the palm of your hand.

What is that?

After a routine cat scan, the doctor found 18 yeast balls (black spots) growing on my daughter's brain. They had never seen this before. Janiece was later diagnosed with Hydrocephalus (cerebrospinal fluid CSF occurs within the brain). Eventually, the doctor placed a ventriculoperitoneal (VP) shunt in her brain to keep the fluid draining properly. The doctors told me that if my daughter survived the surgeries, she might be a vegetable and not be able to walk or talk. My daughter Janiece underwent ten brain operations in her first year of life.

It felt like it would never end! From 1995 - 1997, my daughter had a plethora of surgeries and doctor visits because her shunt kept malfunctioning. The doctors had surgically moved her shunt from the front, back and side of her head trying to find a good placement so the fluid in her brain could flow properly. With all of the surgeries and test that the doctors were doing on my daughter I felt numb and detached from the world. I didn't know if she would live from day to day. I prayed often that God would heal my baby and continue to provide for us. Being a single mother, balancing a business, and caring for a sick child all at the same time left me in a state of bewilderment.

My hair

By 1998 I started feeling tingling in my head. I knew that I was living with Chronic stress, but I was not expecting my hair to fall out. I remember going to bed one night and waking up the next morning to find a bald spot the size of a dime at the nape of my neck. I didn't know what was going on. I had my barber friend cut my hair even in the back so it would not be noticed.

October 13, 1999, my daughter underwent another emergency surgery because she had contracted an infection in her shunt. My baby had a 5% chance of living had she not had the surgery. That was a tremendous amount of stress on me. After that surgery, I started noticing more of my hair falling out. My hair looked like a thief snuck into my room at night and erased the hair right off my scalp. I felt robbed and violated. I could not understand what was going on because I never saw my hair in my comb, brush, or pillow. My hair just disappeared off my scalp and body. My eyebrows fell out within 24 hours, and shortly thereafter, my eyelashes were gone. I realized my nose hairs fell out after a never-ending drip of mucous that I could not wipe away. I went from bald spots to losing all of the hair on my body.

When I looked in the mirror, I did not recognize the person looking back at me. I looked like a monster. Where was Jamie? Who was this person? I did not feel like a woman. I felt like my femininity had been stolen. My God, what is happening to me?

The fear and shame almost paralyzed me. I was scared; here I was - a hairstylist servicing clients, but I could not fix myself. I began to hide and cover up. The masquerade began by accessorizing, applying makeup, wigs, hats, and head wraps because that allowed me to stay numb to the reality of losing my hair. My family, clients, and friends were unaware of my daily struggles.

2004

I finally went to the doctor in 2004 because I only had a few strands of hair on my scalp. I looked and felt like I was dying. I was diagnosed with Alopecia Areata (an autoimmune disease that causes hair loss on the scalp, face, and on other areas of the body). At that point, I felt like my life was over!

The doctor suggested steroid injections in my scalp which were very painful. All the hair growth treatments were proven to be unsuccessful.

The mental struggle, anxiety, panic attacks, depression, weight gain, and weight loss were like a tornado that swirled me around with no end of ever stopping.

My secret

I shied away from relationships because of the insecurities that I had with Alopecia. The thought of sharing my hair loss with a man scared me. One evening I attended a jazz concert and met a nice guy. We had a conversation and laughed together as if we had known each other for years. To my surprise we started a relationship. This guy was amazing and treated me like a queen. Six months had passed, and he did not know my secret. I had managed to hide and give him the impression that all the different hairstyles that I wore were because I was a hairstylist, and that's what we do. The time had come, and the truth had to be revealed. I remember sitting on his living room floor, scared and afraid because I thought he would break off the relationship and not accept me for who I was. I rolled around on the floor, holding my head wrap tight and saying I have to show you what's really going on under this scarf. With my eyes closed, I pulled my scarf off, and he said, "Oh, just cut it." He sat me down on the bathroom toilet and he cut the remaining strands of hair off my head. I was in shock! He looked at me and said you are beautiful! This man loved and affirmed me. Both of us were bald, and my presumption of receiving love because I had Alopecia was wrong. Out in public he always held my hand and greeted me with a kiss. I knew that I was worthy of being loved.

It's bigger than me

I was introduced to an 11-year-old girl who was struggling with Alopecia. The tears fell as she explained she had never seen anyone that looked like her. In that moment, I knew representation matters. I shared a few accessorizing tips and techniques and helped her understand that she was not alone. My heart was heavy, and I cried. I asked God, "What do you want me to do?" He spoke to my heart and told me to start a support group. The Alopecia Support Group was founded in 2009.

The healing journey…

As a woman and hairstylist my biggest struggle was not being able to fix myself. Yes, I wanted my hair to grow back but in reality, I never knew if it would. Alopecia is a rollercoaster ride of emotions and physical changes; it will take you out if you let it. I was not going to let Alopecia kill me mentally, spiritually, or physically. I told myself that I wanted to live and be happy.

As I began to create, support, and provide a safe space for men, women, and children living with Alopecia, I had to heal before I could help someone else. My healing was more than the amount of hair that I loss. God revealed to me that I needed to deal with some past issues in my life. I could no longer hide the anger, insecurities, unforgiveness, low self-esteem, rape, and molestation. Jamie had to face herself and God in the mirror. The mirror does not lie it tells the truth by showing the reflection of whatever stands in front of it. I made the decision to work on myself and change the reflection of what I saw, so I could heal and walk in FREEDOM.

My personal conversations (self-talk) were vital on my healing journey. I was determined to win the fight and empower myself and others. The lack of hair could not and did not determine who I was as a woman. I was more than my hair!

These are the steps I took for my healing that may help you in yours...

1. I asked God for direction
2. I started the Alopecia Support Group
3. I found a counselor/therapist
4. I started exercising and changing my eating habits.
5. I learned how to listen to my body and respond in a healthy way

6. I learned how to say NO.
7. I learned accessorizing techniques (Hats, head wraps, scarves, makeup application and etc.)
8. I had to accept the fact that I may or may not grow my hair back.
9. I educated myself on the disease.
10. I created safe spaces for my Alopecia community to heal and support each other

To this day, I have good days and bad days. I choose to stay focused and walk in the purpose of God. Now I understand that I had to go through all of the pain and disappointment of losing my hair so I could help someone else. My pain has been turned into my purpose!

Remember that everyone has a story, but our story is not for us. It's for someone else!

TELL YOUR STORY!

ALOPECIA: OUR STORIES

I Live the Bald Life!

Meet Jamie Elmore

~ *The Visionary* ~

Jamie Elmore is a hairstylist and salon owner of JSalon in Seattle, WA, and has worked in the industry for 31 years. After her initial diagnosis in 2004, she was incredibly surprised by the lack of resources available for a worldwide epidemic. Striving to regain normalcy in her life, she began dreaming, planning, and becoming a resource for what she wished was accessible when she was dealing with Alopecia's post-traumatic effects and her firsthand hair loss experiences.

She aims to tackle the issue of Alopecia and give a voice to men, women, and children worldwide who suffer in silence. Understanding that 147 million people worldwide suffer from Alopecia, the need became critical and global. Thus, Alopecia Support Group was born in 2009. Jamie began creating innovative ways of healing that include but are not limited to retreats, one-on-one, and group coaching, writing, team building, exercise, Image and Accessory workshops, and global pen pals.

Jamie began writing as a hair loss columnist for three publications, CKW- The Chea K. Woolfolk Magazine, Presidential Style Magazine, and The Seattle Medium newspaper and has been a guest on several radio shows and podcasts. Jamie was also honored to be featured on the cover of Courageous Woman Magazine 2018.

In 2020 Jamie became the Editor in Chief of Bald Life Magazine, where she features Men, Women, and Children from all walks of life that are living with hair loss due to Alopecia, Cancer, medically induced, or simply by choice. The Magazine is a global platform for bald individuals to heal, find their voice, and share their stories. Bald Life Magazine is the first to cater to the hair loss and bald community. Bald Life Magazine is circulating in fifteen countries around the globe.

Jamie is a certified Hair replacement specialist. The founder of the Bald Boss Community, the visionary & creator of the Alopecia Anthology Series and books, (*Alopecia His Story and Alopecia Our Stories Living a Bald Life*), a motivational speaker, Alopecia confidence coach, radio producer, Executive Producer of the Award-winning Documentary "Harmony Alopecia Stories", an advocate, healer, and mentor. Jamie received the Legacy Builder award 2019 and the Soul Café publisher of the year award 2021 and was featured on the Emmy Award-winning show Red Table Talk.

Connect with the Visionary:

Websites:

www.Baldlifemagazine.com

www.baldbosscommunity.com

http://jamierelmore.com

www.alopeciasupportgroup.org

Grab Her First Anthology - Alopecia: His Story: https://www.amazon.com

Harmony Alopecia Stories: (Amazon Prime Video): https://www.primevideo.com/detail/Harmony-Alopecia-Stories

Social Media Platforms

https://www.facebook.com/jamie.elmore.9

https://www.facebook.com/BaldLifeMagazine

https://www.facebook.com/alopeciasupportgroup

https://www.facebook.com/baldbosscommunity

https://instagram.com/jamie.elmore

https://instagram.com/baldlifemagazine

https://instagram.com/baldbosscommunity

https://instagram.com/alopeciasupportgroup

https://youtube.com/@BaldLifeTV

Reference websites:

- www.healthline.com
- www.aad.org
- www.naaf.org

Made in the USA
Middletown, DE
13 May 2023